Reality-Centered People Management

Reality-Centered People Management

Key to Improved Productivity

Erwin S. Stanton

amacom

A Division of American Management Associations

To my parents
with appreciation and gratitude

Library of Congress Cataloging in Publication Data

Stanton, Erwin Schoenfeld.
  Reality-centered people management.

  Bibliography: p.
  Includes index.
  1. Employee motivation.   2. Labor productivity.
3. Management.   I. Title.
HF5549.5.M63S69   658.3′14   81-69368
ISBN 0-8144-5676-6   AACR2

First Printing

Preface

Perhaps the most worrisome problem facing American business today is that of low employee work productivity. The situation is aggravated further as the rate of decline in employee productivity appears to be increasing, particularly in comparison with that of foreign workers. Needless to say, the repercussions are ominous. For every company where productivity fails to keep pace with constantly rising labor costs, profitability and, indeed, the company's very survival may be seriously threatened. For the country as a whole, the consequences may very likely be a general decline in our standard of living, in our individual life styles, and in America's standing, prestige, and influence throughout the world.

What has caused this disturbing dilemma? Many managers and executives report that a major contributor to decline in employee productivity is the drop in individual motivation—the lessening of "the will to work." There has also been a dramatic decline in loyalty to the company and in commitment to the work ethic in general.

Others have challenged this interpretation, citing the numerous findings that have emanated from the behavioral sciences for many years. These findings, they contend, strongly demonstrate that people basically *want* to work, that they want to be truly productive and contribute significantly to their organizations, and that they strive to achieve personal fulfillment and intrinsic satisfaction through their work. These same supporters of what might be called the "motivational school" argue that if employee productivity is found wanting, then surely management has failed to properly apply current behavioral science findings to the work situation.

What is the *real* answer? Why *is* employee productivity declining? Could it be that the behavioral scientists and their motivational theories are, in fact, wrong? Is it just possible that people don't *really* want to work—that they will work only if they absolutely must, and even then, not too well? How can these two sharply contrasting viewpoints on employee motivation and work behavior even be explained, much less reconciled? And most importantly, as a means of resolving the productivity dilemma, what practical and useful recommendations can be offered to operating managers and executives to help them run effective, successful, productive departments and improve the performance of their people?

As an industrial and organizational psychologist, operating executive, and management consultant, I have come to believe that the highly respected behavioral scientists and their renowned theories about employee behavior and motivation are only *partially* correct. The currently popular motivational concepts they have formulated are drastically influenced by many situational and operational factors that significantly limit their acceptance and, more important, their overall applicability. Many practicing managers are also quite correct when, as a result of their own day-in-and-day-out, hands-on observation of the actual behavior of people on the job, they regretfully conclude that employee work motivation and productivity have indeed declined, and that some people simply do not really want to work.

What, then, is the thrust of this book? Basically, I have two distinct objectives. The first is to critically evaluate some of the more popular employee behavior and motivational concepts that have reigned supreme in many management circles for the past several years and to examine both the circumstances and conditions under which such concepts may work and also, perhaps more notably, those under which they may not work very well, if at all.

My second objective is an outgrowth of the first: to offer a comprehensive management system, which I call *Reality-Centered Management,* that will help managers and executives direct the activities of their people in a more effective and results-oriented manner. This system which, in my opinion, clearly and accurately reflects the current realities of business and industry, is intended to strengthen the vitality of our nation's companies and organizations, increase the rate of their "people productivity," and improve employees' commitment to excellence in job performance.

This book is intended for managers and executives who, regardless of organizational level and functional specialty, supervise and direct the work activities of people in profit or nonprofit settings. The book will provide readers with a more useful and concrete strategy to help them improve the performance of their people—not in an idealized or perfect work setting which is rarely found, but rather in the very real world in which managers and executives must function.

I would like at this time to express my appreciation to my wife, Inge Stanton, for her insightful and valuable comments and for acting as a sounding board, and to Ray Vogler for graciously contributing several original light-

Preface

hearted cartoons. My thanks also to Dr. John C. Alexion, Dean of the College of Business Administration of St. John's University, and to Dr. Michael J. Kavanagh, Chairman of the Department of Management, for having granted me a one-year research leave from teaching responsibilities to permit me to write this book. And finally, my appreciation to my secretary, Mrs. Helen Lennon, for her dedicated and conscientious efforts in preparing the manuscript.

ERWIN S. STANTON

Contents

Contents

1
The Productivity
Problem

❧

**Productivity: The average output per employee
per hour of work.**

Productivity. The lifeline of every company and of every
country. Everyone recognizes how essential productivity is
to the effectiveness and profitability of a company. Indeed,
it determines the very success or failure of both businesses
and nonprofit organizations. In a broader sense, however,
productivity dramatically affects the strength, influence,
viability, and national security of our country itself and the
overall well-being of its citizens. Hence, an ever rising level
of productivity is absolutely essential if companies are to
grow and thrive and if our standard of living, which is the
envy of the world, and the life styles Americans have
striven to attain over the past years are to be maintained.

This concept is neither new nor startling. All well-
managed companies, as well as government administra-
tions over the years, have always been concerned with finding and developing ways of improving productivity levels.
And while top organizational executives have long been
committed to designing and implementing comprehensive
systems, technology, and strategies for productivity im-

provement, the importance of productivity has not been lost on individual managers and supervisors. In fact, at their level of responsibility, all managers are acutely aware of the distinct difference between a department that traditionally meets its goals and objectives successfully and a department that continually fails to do so because of serious obstacles and difficulties—that difference being the rate of productivity achieved. As a result, both managers and staff specialists are constantly seeking ways to improve the productivity of their departments.

Throughout its history, the United States has had virtually no problem increasing its rate of industrial productivity as well as maintaining its competitive edge vis-à-vis other nations. Indeed, our country has long been—and basically still is—the envy of the world because of our overall industrial efficiency and our impressive and continually rising productivity level. With this success has come, for the vast majority of Americans, a comfortable standard of living—one to which other countries aspire.

More recently, something has gone seriously wrong. Impressive as our *historical* industrial gains have been—and despite the fact that our overall current productivity level is still the highest in the world—for some time now our rate of productivity *growth* has faltered and significantly declined, particularly in comparison with that of many foreign countries. In the wake of this drop in productivity growth have come serious repercussions for numerous industries and companies as well as for the nation's economy as a whole and notably for our international trade balance.

Indeed, in recent years our newspapers and business magazines increasingly and with considerable alarm have drawn attention to the magnitude of the productivity growth problem.* We are regularly confronted with an

---

* For an excellent comprehensive review of the productivity problem, see "The Reindustrialization of America," *Business Week*, June 30, 1980, pp. 56–142.

outpouring of negative, pessimistic, and disquieting statistics underscoring the seriousness of the issue and its grave implications for the future. Note, for example, some recently reported findings:

o While over the past 30 years productivity grew at the rate of 2.8 percent per year, during the past 10 years the rate declined by .5 to 1.5 percent per year. (Source: U.S. Department of Labor)

o "America's technological edge over other nations has all but disappeared." (Source: *Business Week,* 1980)

o In comparison with six other major industrial nations, the United States ranks with Great Britain as having the lowest rate of productivity gains in the past ten years: 27 percent. In the same period, Japan gained 107 percent and West Germany 70 percent. (Source: *Washington Post,* 1980)

o If the United States had maintained its 1947–67 productivity growth rate of 3.2 percent per year from 1967 onward, our real gross national product would have been $268 billion higher in 1978. (Source: American Productivity Center)

o The Japanese steel worker produces about 420 tons of steel per year as opposed to the American worker's 200–250 tons. (Source: *Money Manager,* March 3, 1980)

o Japanese workers have increased their output by more than three times the annual rate of increase for American workers. (Source: U.S. Department of Labor, 1979)

o Philip Caldwell, Chairman of the Ford Motor Company, pleaded for restrictions on the importation of Japanese cars to protect the American automobile industry. (Source: testimony before the International Trade Commission, Washington, D.C., October 9, 1980)

o "Our national production rate has fallen behind those of other countries because many of them are prepared to make more sacrifices than we are. The workers of Japan, for instance, are motivated by a relentless work ethic. As a nation, they are prepared to work harder . . . to keep goods flowing abroad." (Source: Thomas A. Murphy, Chairman, General Motors Corporation)

o Compensation rose almost 9 percent during 1979, while productivity declined 2 percent. As a consequence, unit labor costs rose 11.5 percent. (Source: *Business Week*, 1980)

o "The average American is likely to see his standard of living drastically decline in the 1980s unless the United States accelerates its rate of productivity growth. Productivity is the linchpin of economic progress in the next decade." (Source: Senator Lloyd Bentsen, D–Texas)

o The American standard of living—the highest in the world as recently as 1972—now ranks in only fifth place. (Source: *Business Week*, 1980)

The decline in American industry's ability to compete effectively overseas is nearly an economic disaster. In recent years, American business has been losing market share at an accelerating rate, not only at home, but also in foreign markets. Note, as just two illustrations, the dominance of Japanese consumer electronic goods and the surge in sales of Japanese cars at the expense of American automobile manufacturers. Overall, the United States actually lost 23 percent of the world market in the 1970s, after a 16 percent decline during the 1960s. *Business Week* estimated that this drop represents some $125 billion in lost production and a loss of approximately 2 million American jobs.

While the United States is still ahead, at least for now, foreign producers are catching up fast. In 1973, the average Japanese worker produced 55 percent of what his or her American counterpart turned out, and the German worker was already up to 74 percent of the American worker's output. By 1979, however, the Japanese employee had moved up to a ratio of 66 percent, and the German worker to 88 percent. Unless our rate of productivity growth drastically improves, *Business Week* estimates that both countries will overtake us by the mid-1980s.

Why Has Productivity Declined?

It is much easier to document the decline of productivity growth than to offer a truly satisfactory explanation for why it is occurring in the first place. In fact, the search for the causes of the productivity decline has confounded, perplexed, and frustrated not only executives and managers but expert economists as well. Many explanations have been suggested, but there is no universal agreement as to the cause. Most observers are convinced, however, that the reasons for the decline are numerous, interrelated, and complex.

Despite the lack of clear consensus on the causes of the problem, everyone *does* agree that if we are to revitalize our economy, to become more competitive not only domestically but also internationally, and to assure our citizens an ever rising standard of living in a society that has come to expect that the "pie" will always increase, then productivity improvement must become a priority of the highest order both for business and for the nation.

What are some of the specific reasons that have been offered to explain the slowdown in productivity? Perhaps the numerous and complex explanations were best synthesized at a recent conference jointly sponsored by the U.S. Senate Subcommittee on International Trade, the New York Stock Exchange, and Harvard University. Among the key causes suggested were the following:

The decline in research and development expenditures.
The decline in the rate of investment in new capital equipment.
The increase in the cost and burden of government regulations.
The rise in energy costs.

The effects of inflation.

The decline in employee motivation and commitment to high-quality work performance.

Clearly the problem—and its corresponding challenge—is enormous. There are no simple solutions, and it is most unlikely that any single proposal can adequately address the problem and achieve the desired results. In all likelihood, the search for a solution will require the combined effort and expertise of knowledgeable specialists from several disciplines.

Productivity and Motivation

I fully recognize and respect the fact that the drop in productivity growth is unquestionably the result of many factors. This book, however, will address itself almost exclusively to the *decline in employee motivation and commitment to work*—one of the *major* causes of the productivity slowdown.

Indeed, it is my contention that one of the most serious problems facing management today is the decline in employee motivation, the marked lessening of the will to work, and the notable drop in employee commitment to the work ethic and to the goals and objectives of the companies that pay their salaries.

No doubt in the course of their duties, all managers have encountered employees who simply are not motivated, who will goof off at the slightest opportunity, and who will only do the absolute minimum needed to keep from being fired. Then, again, as consumers we have all too often come across personnel who do not seem to care, whose work is shoddy, and who appear to be totally lacking in interest, attention, and application.

What is perhaps even more disturbing—especially at a time when we should be looking for ways to *improve* productivity—is the rather cynical attitude on the part of some people who seem to generally disparage work and suggest that there must be something inherently wrong with anyone who subscribes to the work ethic. In fact, the advice given by a whole spate of recent popular magazine articles and by at least one book appears to be that people should be predominantly concerned with the hedonistic pursuit of their own self-indulgent desires and pleasures—that they should "do their own thing," focusing on personal fulfillment and "beating the system," and have only minimal or passing concern for making any sort of contribution to the companies that employ them.

In short, many observers feel that in recent years there has been an alarming increase in the number of employees who have become overly complacent and self-indulgent. Such employees are hardly even interested in the problems and goals of their companies, much less willing to actively lend a hand to the very organizations that keep them on the payroll and make it possible for them to enjoy the standard of living that they have attained and that they fully expect should continue to improve. This, these observers argue, is the crux of the low employee productivity problem.

On the other hand, some people take a drastically different view in assessing the relationship between employee motivation and productivity. These individuals, who may be referred to as the "motivational school," seriously challenge the above explanation of the decline in business productivity. Armed with a host of research studies which they feel absolutely and unequivocally prove their viewpoint, they contend that employee motivation is virtually an inherent human characteristic, and that the overwhelming majority of people basically *want* to work and are interested in making significant contributions to their organizations. They further argue that numerous empirical studies have documented that people seek personal fulfillment and self-actualization through their work. Hence, if employee productivity is unsatisfactory, they contend, the fault lies with management and its failure to pay proper heed to these research findings and appropriately implement the recommendations of behavioral scientists.

Which is the correct answer? Do people *truly* want to work? Are they in fact self-motivated and self-directed? Or is the opposite more typically the case? Which factors and conditions *really* affect the all-important productivity level? And most critically, what specific recommendations can be made to help managers and executives direct the activities of their people, achieve present organizational goals and objectives, and plan for the future growth and viability of their companies.

This book will take a hard look at these basic issues. It will explore and question some of the behavioral concepts about how people can best be directed and motivated that have been recommended to managers over the past years. And it will examine how relevant such recommendations actually are. Finally, the book will offer readers a conceptual model as well as some specific and concrete suggestions for effective management in today's dynamic, difficult, and rapidly changing world as it heads toward the twenty-first century.

Overview of the Book

The present chapter has suggested that one major explanation for the drop in the growth of industrial productivity—albeit not the only one—is the decline in employee motivation. We have also raised the issue of whether or not people really are intrinsically motivated to work, recognizing the inevitable link between work commitment and the productivity problem. What, then, is the subsequent direction of this book?

Chapter 2 will review some of the more popular behavioral and motivational theories about how people are *supposed* to work—theories which have been so widely acclaimed in various business circles for many years. Chapter 3, on the other hand, will explore why these much-heralded motivational theories do not always seem to work, and how various situational and operational factors can prevent their being applied with universal success. In Chapter 4, we shall introduce the concept of *Reality-Centered Management,* a managerial system that will integrate *workable* behavioral and motivational theories with present-day business realities and provide managers with concrete strategies for carrying out their day-in-and-day-out functions more effectively as a means of achieving organizational objectives.

Chapter 5 will explore how the strategies of *Reality-Centered Management* can be implemented by managers on a continuing basis. Included in the specific applications will be: how employee commitment to high-quality performance can be gained, how performance evaluation and management by objectives can be integrated with Reality-Centered Management, and how managers can best establish the necessary degree of discipline in their departments.

Chapter 6 looks to the future and focuses on how a company can make certain it will have sufficiently trained and experienced personnel available to assure the organization's continued growth and viability. Here we will examine some specific tools and techniques for accomplishing this purpose, including organization and human resources planning; the proper use of psychological assessments of key personnel being considered for promotion; and the development of management needs analyses, management inventories, and management succession analyses.

In the book's final chapter, we will recap and summarize the key managerial techniques and strategies most likely to assist managers to properly direct the activities of their people and achieve the goals and objectives of their organizations—not in a hypothetical or idealized world but rather in the actual world of real difficulties which managers must continually confront.

2
Behavioral and Motivational Theories

❦

How Theories Say People Are Supposed to Work

For the past twenty years, managers and executives have been exposed to a vast body of findings that have emanated almost unceasingly from the rapidly growing field of industrial and organizational psychology. Numerous studies, research reports, and well-formulated theories have attempted to explain the complex behavior of people at work and, more importantly, to give practicing managers some rather precise and specific prescriptions for the best way to manage an organization's human resources and thereby optimize a department's productivity.

Indeed, the influence of such applied psychologists as Maslow, McGregor, Herzberg, Likert, and Argyris has been quite formidable, and it is most unlikely that there is a manager today who, at one time or another, has not been thoroughly exposed to some of the "people-management suggestions" offered by these behavioral science "greats." In fact, it is quite difficult to overemphasize the impact that these pioneering industrial-organizational psychologists have had on their professional colleagues by stimulating a vast amount of additional research on the subject of work motivation. The numerous contributions and recommendations made by this rather elite group of psychologists has also had a profound effect on business and industry and has significantly influenced the development and implementation of current organizational policies and practices for the management of human resources.

This chapter will briefly summarize and attempt to bring into clear focus precisely what measures these trend-setting industrial-organizational psychologists have advocated to help managers direct their organizations better. But in order to fully understand their concepts and suggestions, it is also necessary to consider the time frame during which their formulations were developed as well as some of the more significant economic, political, and sociological factors which influenced their thinking.

The 1960s, and to a lesser extent some of the latter part of the 1950s, were fruitful years for the formulation and development of psychological concepts designed to make a contribution to the world of work. In a broader sense, this period unquestionably was heady for American business. In all likelihood, historians will view the soaring sixties as the golden decade in terms of our country's economic growth and development.

The period following the Second World War ushered in an era of unprecedented economic growth as well as individual prosperity for all but the bottom 20 percent of our population. The country witnessed seemingly countless technological advances that significantly increased the disposable income of Americans during a period when inflation was happily relatively contained. As a result, our standard of living was dramatically enhanced, and it seemed that all the material advantages of middle-class living—and possibly even more—were well within most people's reach. In short, the 1960s were characterized by steady and orderly economic prosperity, accompanied by virtually unbridled optimism and confidence in the nation's future.

It was precisely during this time period that some of the

most significant motivational research dealing with the world of work was carried out—research which was to profoundly impact subsequent managerial thinking. Clearly, the industrial psychologists were themselves influenced by events around them, but other significant factors also came into play and helped formulate their ideas. By and large, these pioneering industrial psychologists were powerfully affected by humanistic and ethical values and by a strong concern for the psychological well-being of the individual, no doubt in part, at least, as a result of their own education, general orientation, and personal experience.

Essentially, the various motivational principles put forth by the psychologists were predicated on the implicit understanding that America had a powerful, impressive, and magnificent industrial machine that held out the prospect of considerable prosperity for all our citizens. At the same time, the psychologists believed that people had within them the inherent ability, talent, and latent potential to enable that industrial machine to function in the best possible manner and, consequently, to virtually guarantee economic prosperity and an ever higher national standard of living. All that had to be done to accomplish this illustrious objective was to get managers to implement the motivational concepts offered to them so that their employees would be fully stimulated and challenged to make maximum contributions to their companies.

Let us now examine some of these major motivational concepts which have reigned for so many years.

Maslow's Hierarchy of Needs

Perhaps the first of the more influential behavioralists who focused on the motivational process was the late Abraham H. Maslow.* A clinical psychologist by orientation and at

* A. H. Maslow, *Motivation and Personality*, 2nd ed. (New York: Harper & Row, 1970).

one time president of the American Psychological Association, he spent virtually all his professional life within the relatively sheltered walls of academia. Maslow actually only began applying his concepts to the more practical world of work toward the latter years of his career. Yet his impact on the thinking of contemporary managers and executives has been quite formidable.

Strongly influenced by humanistic values, Maslow believed that, from the beginning of life until the very end, people continually seek the satisfaction of certain needs. That search determines and directs human behavior. Maslow categorized and ranked these needs in ascending order according to their potency, starting with certain basic lower-level, life-sustaining needs and proceeding sequentially to higher-level needs.

The lower-level needs, which Maslow referred to as essentially survival needs, have first call on human behavior. Until these needs are relatively satisfied, higher-level needs cannot be activated. Consequently, according to Maslow, people in their behavior proceed from the satisfaction of lower-level needs to the satisfaction of higher-level needs, following a specific hierarchical order. Furthermore, only once a lower-level need is relatively satisfied do people proceed to satisfy the next level of need. In addition, Maslow stressed that once a lower-level need has been basically satisfied, it loses its potency and therefore no longer motivates. At that point, people will tend to shift their attention up the hierarchy and seek satisfaction of the next higher level need. Maslow listed his hierarchy of needs as follows.

1. *Physiological needs.* The physiological needs are the starting point that determines human behavior. Included here are the basic survival needs for food, water, shelter, sleep, and other physical essentials. Clearly, unless these most fundamental needs are met, people cannot strive for the satisfaction of any higher needs. Hungry people must first eat before they can focus their attention on anything

else. In our society, money is, of course, the medium that makes it possible to satisfy the basic needs of life.

2. *Safety needs.* According to Maslow, once the physiological needs have been reasonably satisfied, people then proceed to satisfy the next higher level need—that of assuring they are relatively safe from the dangers and insecurities of their environment. Once again, money generally enables people to satisfy this fundamental need.

3. *Need for belongingness.* The belongingness need involves people's desire for social interaction—the need to belong to groups, affiliate with other people, and be accepted by those with whom one associates. This need also tends to be readily satisfied in our society through the very act of working—that is, by dealing with others in a job context.

4. *Need for esteem.* The first three needs in Maslow's hierarchy are basic or "deficit" needs. As previously indicated, however, once these fundamental needs have been satisfied, people become motivated to seek satisfaction of higher-level needs. The first of the higher-level needs is that of ego or esteem, a need which Maslow subdivided into two aspects. The first aspect is people's need to experience self-worth, competence, and mastery in their primary areas of activity; the second is people's need for appreciation, recognition, and respect from others.

5. *Need for self-actualization.* The need for self-actualization represents the highest level toward which humans strive. After all the lower-level needs have been satisfied, people are now motivated toward the fulfillment of their ultimate inner selves or, as Maslow termed it, ". . . to become everything that one is capable of becoming." Stated another way, self-actualized persons feel they have truly achieved their full potential.

Maslow contended that under current business conditions most American employees already have their lower-level or deficit needs substantially satisfied. Therefore, such managerial strategies as increasing employees' incomes, strengthening their job security, or enhancing their feelings of social satisfaction would not accomplish any worthwhile purpose. They would not really further employees' actual job satisfaction nor improve organizational productivity. Only by achieving self-esteem and ultimately satisfying the need for self-actualization through their work would employees be truly fulfilled.

Moreover, and of particular practical interest to com-

...WOULD YOU MIND GROVELLING AND WHIMPERING A BIT? – MONEY ALONE DOESN'T BRING THE JOB SATISFACTION IT ONCE DID.

Courtesy of Ray Vogler
Printed with permission

15

panies, only when individuals do the type of work that leads to the satisfaction of their unique needs for esteem and ultimately for self-actualization would they be able to make notable contributions to their organizations. Consequently, it was clearly in both the individual's and the company's interest for jobs to be so structured as to enable employees to strive toward the ultimate satisfaction of their self-actualization need. Only when such conditions prevailed could companies make optimum use of their human resources.

McGregor's Theory X and Theory Y

The industrial psychologist who has probably had the greatest impact on management thinking during the 1960s and 1970s was the late Douglas McGregor. A prominent behavioralist who had written, lectured, and consulted widely with business and industry, he achieved a recognition within the business community generally unmatched by his colleagues, perhaps because of the clarity and succinctness with which he expressed his ideas. McGregor, who was Sloan Professor of Management at the Massachusetts Institute of Technology at the time of his death, published his far-reaching recommendations for management practice in *The Human Side of Enterprise,** which The Conference Board reports has been read by more business people and influenced them more than any other book.

McGregor believed that managers' styles of leading and directing people are very closely related to their belief systems. In expanding this idea, McGregor offered two diametrically opposed theoretical constructs or fundamental assumptions regarding the behavior of people at work. He termed them *Theory X* and *Theory Y*. According to Theory X, which McGregor described as the more traditional management view that calls for firm direction and

* New York: McGraw-Hill, 1960.

close control over personnel, average employees basically inherently dislike work, prefer to be directed by superiors, wish to avoid responsibility, are relatively unambitious, are unconcerned about their companies, and are primarily motivated by the need for security. Consequently, managers who subscribe to these assumptions about how people function in the world of work are apt to exhibit quite a limited and restricted leadership style. They will manage their employees by resorting to coercion, fear, and threats of punishment, while simultaneously implementing an elaborate control system to keep employees under constant surveillance and make certain that organizational objectives are attained.

McGregor admitted that under Theory X type of management a certain amount of reasonably effective work does get done. However, he stressed that, as a rule, this approach was only likely to achieve *minimal* results, at best. Instead, he pleaded for a more contemporary approach to management, namely Theory Y, which he felt would respond more readily to employees' emotional needs while achieving far greater organizational effectiveness. Theory Y rests on the following basic assumptions:

1. The expenditure of physical and mental effort in work is as natural as play or rest. Depending upon a variety of conditions, work can either be a source of satisfaction and will accordingly be willingly performed, or it can be a source of punishment and will if possible be avoided.
2. External control and the threat of punishment are not management's only means of stimulating employee effort toward achieving organizational objectives. Employees will exercise self-direction and self-control to reach objectives to which they are personally committed.
3. Commitment to objectives can be achieved through the satisfaction of employee's ego and self-actualization needs.
4. The average person can learn to not only accept but to actively seek responsibility.

17

5. The capacity to demonstrate imagination, ingenuity and creativity and apply them to solving organizational problems is widely, not narrowly, distributed in the work population.
6. Under the conditions of modern industrial life, the intellectual potential of the average employee is only partially used.

Readers will quickly recognize that McGregor's thinking closely paralleled Maslow's in his emphasis on the importance of satisfying ego and self-actualization needs. However, his prominence as the leading spokesman for the industrial psychology of his day perhaps resulted from his having gone one step beyond Maslow by offering a blueprint for implementation. McGregor stressed that if organizations basically subscribe to Theory Y style of management, they will be rewarded on the bottom line by being much more successful in attaining organizational objectives. How was management to implement Theory Y to achieve such practical results? Here McGregor clearly spelled out specific strategies, urging managers to delegate more responsibility to employees, broaden their areas of work activity, and allow people to participate more actively in matters directly affecting them on the job.

Herzberg's Motivation–Hygiene Theory

The most influential of the current industrial-organizational psychologists is unquestionably Frederick Herzberg, presently Distinguished Professor of Management at the University of Utah, who proposed the Motivation-Hygiene Theory.* Indeed, his impact on the thinking of business executives and managers over the past twenty years has been phenomenal: without doubt his is the first name business people associate with the field of

---

* *Work and the Nature of Man* (Cleveland: World Publishing Company, 1966).

industrial-organizational psychology in general and the topic of work motivation in particular.

Herzberg's success can probably be attributed to three factors: He is a clear and succinct writer who expresses himself in a way that the business community can readily understand; he has a rather dynamic personality that has resulted in his becoming a much sought after speaker and organizational consultant; and his motivational theory has provided the conceptual foundation for the currently popular job-enrichment movement, which will be discussed later in this chapter. This is not to say that Herzberg does not have his critics.* If anything, it is because his theory has generated so much controversy and given rise to so many subsequent cross-cultural research studies to determine the generalizability of his findings and conclusions that there exists today such extensive and growing professional literature on work motivation.

Paramount to the Motivation-Hygiene Theory is the idea that two sets of factors are operative in any job situation: satisfiers and dissatisfiers. However, these satisfiers and dissatisfiers do not represent opposite ends of the *same* continuum, but rather are completely *different* factors. Thus, in the work situation, the absence of the specific factors that lead to job satisfaction does not generate job *dis*satisfaction, but merely *non*satisfaction.

The factors resulting in job satisfaction that Herzberg called "motivators" are related to a job's intrinsic *content*. They include achievement, recognition, the nature of the work itself, responsibility, advancement, and a feeling of personal growth. Accordingly, Herzberg argued that people who do not feel challenged or stimulated by their work are not dissatisfied but only not satisfied.

Conversely, those aspects of a work situation leading to·

* Interested readers may wish to consult Robert J. House and Lawrence A. Wigdor, "Herzberg's Dual-Factor Theory of Job Satisfaction and Motivation: A Review of the Evidence and a Criticism," *Personnel Psychology*, Winter 1967, pp. 369–89.

job dissatisfaction that Herzberg called "hygiene factors" are related to a job's extrinsic *context*. They include such considerations as company policy and administration, supervision, working conditions, job security, and—

...AS A MOTIVATIONAL CONCEPT IT'S REALLY QUITE FOOLPROOF, FROBISHER

Courtesy of Ray Vogler
Printed with permission

perhaps the most controversial item of all—salary. Accordingly, Herzberg stressed that people who are unhappy with their pay would be dissatisfied; should their salary subsequently be increased to what they felt it should be, they would not then become satisfied, but merely not dissatisfied. Drawing an analogy with Maslow's concepts, Herzberg likened Maslow's lower-level needs to his hygiene factors, while the ego and self-actualization needs corresponded to his motivators.

Crucial to the Motivation-Hygiene Theory was the idea that only when people experience true job satisfaction—that is, when the motivators are activated—are they really stimulated to do high-quality work and thereby make worthwhile contributions to their companies. Yet, Herzberg argued, most of management's efforts focus on the hygiene factors—that is, on removing those elements that lead to job dissatisfaction. While stressing the importance of paying attention to these lower-level needs and removing the dissatisfiers, he noted that such a strategy would only eliminate employee dissatisfaction without really motivating people toward extra effort. Instead, far more impressive results would be achieved if companies were to redesign or enrich the content of work and build motivators into jobs, for only when such conditions prevail will organizations really function in a truly productive manner. Since Herzberg linked motivation so inextricably to productivity, it is easy to understand his pervasive influence on management thinking.

Emphasis on Participative Management

In the motivational theories discussed so far in this chapter, the behavioralists have emphasized the importance of the nature and content of work as a means of spurring employees to greater productivity. A related concept is that of employee participation. Although many industrial-organizational psychologists have emphasized the need for greater employee participation, two behavioralists in particular can be singled out for their prominence in this area.

Chris Argyris, of the Harvard University Graduate School of Business, has long felt that many factors, particularly various control mechanisms, found in modern business organizations make demands on employees which are inconsistent with the needs of mature adults.* The result, he feels, is frequently either employee apathy, disinterest, and noninvolvement (an "I don't care" attitude, if you will) or a variety of aggressive and hostile employee behaviors, either covert or overt. The responses are, in either case, clearly counterproductive to the aims of the organization. To overcome this type of dysfunctional behavior and optimize human resources, Argyris has urged the intergration of organizational and individual needs through the introduction of programs of job enlargement and employee participation.

Similarly, Rensis Likert and his associates, who for many years conducted some rather elaborate research studies at the Institute for Social Research of the University of Michigan, have stressed the superiority of a highly participative group approach as a means of enhancing individual job satisfaction and increasing organizational productivity.†

The Job Redesign Movement

A major part of the recommendations and motivational theories of the behavioral scientists has found its way into what for the last 15 years has become known as the "job

---

* Chris Argyris, *Integrating the Individual and the Organization* (New York: John Wiley & Sons, 1964).
† Rensis Likert, *The Human Organization* (New York: McGraw-Hill, 1967).

redesign movement."* Indeed, much has been written about job redesign, extolling its many virtues and suggesting that it is the elusive panacea that will solve an organization's many problems. Numerous articles have appeared in business magazines as well as in the popular press promising that the introduction of a job redesign program will have the happy effect of simultaneously increasing both a company's productivity and the job satisfaction of its employees.

Job redesign applications can be classified into three categories: job rotation, job enlargement, and the most popular and most widely discussed, job enrichment. Actually, however, many observers note that job rotation and job enlargement are really nothing new. These techniques have been known to both managers and industrial engineers for many years, certainly since before the emergence of the behavioral scientists. Job rotation is essentially no more than moving employees through a series of departments or assignments as a means of increasing their versatility. The approach may offer the added benefit of reducing employees' boredom by exposing them to a changing work environment. Job enlargement calls for expanding people's duties by diversifying and broadening their tasks and thereby reducing the repetitiveness of merely performing a single or limited number of relatively isolated and unrelated functions.

Job enrichment, which is regarded as the practical embodiment of current motivational concepts, is completely different. Based fundamentally on Frederick Herzberg's Motivation-Hygiene Theory, it aims to drastically reorganize jobs so as to increase productivity and enhance individual satisfaction. The assumption underlying job enrichment is that motivation and productivity are inex-

* For further information, see Harold M. F. Rush, *Job Design for Motivation* (New York: The Conference Board, 1971); see also some of the current publications of the Work in America Institute, Inc., Scarsdale, N.Y.

tricably linked. Hence, for productivity to rise, individuals must be motivated. Motivation, however, will not exist unless employees derive a feeling of satisfaction from their work and, in addition, have a certain degree of freedom and autonomy on the job. Therefore, say Herzberg and his supporters, jobs must be redesigned or "enriched." Job enrichment cannot be accomplished by improving such "hygiene factors" as pay, benefits, or working conditions. Only by building satisfiers or motivators right into jobs will motivation, and hence productivity, really rise. Consequently, in redesigning jobs, Herzberg's six motivators (achievement, recognition, the nature of the work performed, responsibility, advancement, and personal growth) must become an intrinsic part of people's work.

How can job enrichment be successfully implemented in a company? Herzberg offers the following specific guidelines.*

1. Remove some of the controls on employees while at the same time retaining managerial accountability.
2. Increase individual employees' accountability for their own work.
3. Give employees a complete natural unit of work, not just fragmented and isolated tasks.
4. Give employees additional authority in their work activities, thereby increasing job freedom and autonomy.
5. Periodically make reports directly available to employees, rather than only to their supervisors.
6. Introduce new and more difficult tasks to the job.
7. Assign specific or specialized tasks to employees, thereby enabling them to become experts in their work.

A number of organizations, including AT&T, General Foods, Texas Instruments, Corning Glass Works, and

* Frederick Herzberg, "One More Time: How Do You Motivate Employees?" *Harvard Business Review*, January–February 1968, pp. 53–62.

TRW, have enthusiastically embraced the job-enrichment concept and attempted to implement such programs within their own companies.* Readers will immediately ask, of course, how job enrichment has worked out. Has it justified the expectations of its supporters and have the promised results materialized? Chapter 3 will respond to these questions, and I shall ask readers' patience until then.

Summary

The present chapter has summarized and highlighted the key motivational theories about how people are *supposed* to work and how organizations can make the best use of human resources to achieve their goals and objectives. The theories discussed have received considerable recognition and acceptance in many quarters. Nevertheless, in view of the problem of our nation's declining productivity, examined in Chapter 1, the paramount question that must be raised is how valid, realistic, and workable are these motivational theories. This will be dealt with in the following chapter.

---

* Readers interested in job enrichment might wish to consult the following books: Robert N. Ford, *Motivation Through the Work Itself* (New York: American Management Associations, 1969); M. Scott Myers, *Every Employee A Manager* (New York: McGraw-Hill, 1970); *Work in America*, Report of a Special Task Force to the Secretary of Health, Education and Welfare (Boston: MIT Press, 1972); and J. Richard Hackman and Greg R. Oldham, *Work Redesign* (Reading, Mass.: Addison-Wesley, 1980)

3
Behavioral
and Motivational
Theories

❧

Why People Don't Always Work
as Theories Say They Should

The preceding chapter reviewed the major employee motivational concepts to which American managers have been exposed for many years. There may be certain discrepancies and perhaps some inconsistencies among the theories, but the essential message for practicing managers is fairly clear: People are basically motivated toward work and generally have the ability and desire to be productive and to contribute tangibly to the attainment of organizational goals and objectives. Management, for its part, possesses the knowledge, expertise, and capability to make full use of this inherent productive capacity in such a way as to meet organizational criteria for success and at the same time fulfill the job satisfaction needs of employees. If anticipated employee productivity is found wanting, then surely the problem can be attributed to management's failure to properly apply current behavioral science findings to the work situation.

However, many seasoned managers, including those who have been trained in all the popular motivational theories, are quite uncomfortable whenever they hear these principles enthusiastically endorsed. The concepts might indeed sound very good in theory, but their own experiences have shown that in practice the principles simply do not always work well. In fact, at times, they do not work at all. As a result, these managers see a dramatic inconsistency between the theories and recommendations so convincingly put forth by the "motivational school" and the stark reality of the practical world of work and management in which they must function daily.

Going a step further, every manager has encountered more than just a handful of employees who simply are not motivated, and who consistently fail to perform at a satisfactory level, despite management's best efforts to implement the behavioralists' recommendations for improvement. No doubt readers, in their roles as consumers, have also had their own firsthand experience with employees who simply do not care, and whose attitude can only be described as "I just work here."

What About Job Enrichment?

As we have seen in the preceding chapter, job enrichment has been touted by behavioral scientists as the vehicle for implementing the motivational principles that have been suggested to both improve organizational productivity and to enhance employee job satisfaction. The principle behind job enrichment is that only by building into the job Herzberg's satisfiers or motivators—that is, achievement, recognition, interest in the work itself, responsibility, advancement, and personal growth—will individuals be truly motivated and hence able to contribute meaningfully toward attainment of the company's goals. Indeed, for the past ten years, we have heard so much about the alleged marvels of job enrichment that it has almost come to be regarded as a magic wand which will give us the elusive productivity we all want.

How *has* job enrichment actually fared? Has it really worked? Has it been so overwhelmingly successful that it should be unequivocally recommended for implementation on a broad scale? Reports from organizations that have explored and implemented job enrichment programs are mixed; results have varied widely.* Moreover, truly objective outside evaluations are hard to come by, and it is often difficult to completely isolate job enrichment experiments from other developments simultaneously occurring in the organization and in society. Some companies report they have been satisfied; others note disappointing results; still others inaugurated job enrichment programs enthusiastically and with great publicity, only to disband them quietly and without fanfare later on.

Some managers who support the job enrichment concept have reported that turnover, absenteeism, and employee complaints have generally gone down, while quality, productivity, and morale have gone up. Other managers, however, have experienced inconclusive or even negative results and have discontinued their job enrichment efforts. In some instances, job enrichment actually caused a decline in productivity that could not be made up, even with time: the benefits never did outweigh the costs.† Interestingly, although job enrichment is supposed to appeal to higher-level needs, many employees have not taken to the program, preferring more traditional work arrangements that require less individual responsibility and provide them with more job structure.‡ To add to the difficulties, union leaders in organized com-

* J. Richard Hackman and Greg R. Oldham, *Work Redesign* (Reading, Mass.: Addison-Wesley, 1980).
† Antone F. Alber, "The Real Cost of Job Enrichment," *Business Horizons*, February 1979, pp. 60–7$. For a critical review of job enrichment, see M. Fein, "Job Enrichment: A Reevaluation," *Sloan Management Review*, Winter 1974, pp. 69–88.
‡ *A Work Experiment: Six Americans in a Swedish Plant* (New York: The Ford Foundation, 1976).

panies have not always been enthusiastic about job enrichment programs and indeed frequently have appeared
distrustful of management's purpose.*

In view of these results, is it possible at this point to
evaluate the overall effectiveness of job enrichment? Probably it is too early to draw definitive conclusions, and business will simply need more time to fully evaluate programs
currently in operation as well as those in the planning
stages. It would appear, however, that while job enrichment might be one suitable option that management could
introduce selectively, it probably is not the panacea that
has been claimed.

Have Motivational Theories
Really Weathered Close Scrutiny?

In the final analysis, how valid, realistic, and universal *are*
the highly acclaimed motivational principles? Do they
really hold up under most circumstances and in most work
situations? Perhaps even more important, is the practicing
manager well advised to institute the various recommendations put forth by behavioral scientists as a means of
spurring employees to greater productivity? Or, as with
job enrichment, are we merely dealing with humanistic,
but utopian, theories of a world as it should be and as it is
seen through the eyes of idealists, rather than looking at
hard reality? Could it just be that the motivationalists and
their theories are basically wrong after all? Clearly, these
are critical questions that require a definitive answer. We
will attempt to provide one in this chapter.

The answer to the question of whether motivational
theories have withstood close scrutiny is quite complex and
does not come easily. In evaluating all the evidence—both
from empirical research as well as from reports of the

* For a union view of job enrichment, see William W. Winpisinger, "Job Satisfaction: A Union Response," *American Federationist*, February 1973, pp. 8-10.

practical, hands-on experience of managers throughout the country in differing work settings—the results are quite mixed. Yes, at times, the motivational theories do work, and very well, enabling an organization to function quite effectively. And no, at times, the motivational principles do not really hold up in practice, and as a consequence, many managers who attempted to implement them have become disappointed and sadly disillusioned. The motivationalists, at the same time, insist that their findings and principles are essentially universal and accordingly claim emphatically that they should hold up. How, then, can the discrepancies in the results be satisfactorily explained?

If there were an easy answer, there probably would be no need for this book. Obviously, the explanation is complex and involves many diverse circumstances affecting the motivational process. I believe, however, that the confusion, discrepancies, and paradox surrounding the entire work motivation issue can be clarified by a more thorough examination of the following three factors, which will be fully explored in this chapter:

1. The degree of work motivation varies rather widely among people.
2. Within the past decade, there has been a significant change in the attitudes of many employees toward work.
3. The expansion of various government social support programs has contributed significantly to changes in employee work motivation and productivity.

People's Work Motivation Varies Widely

As we have seen in the previous chapter, behavioral scientists appear to be virtually unanimous in their opinion that work per se is a very strong human drive and that most people seek maximum personal fulfillment through the act of working. In fact, scientists go so far as to say that the job is the *main* focus of many people's lives, and that, for such dedicated individuals, true fulfillment can come about only through the achievement of on-the-job satisfaction. Indeed, to a great extent, the "motivational school" has taken on a certain evangelical aspect, with behavioralists widely extolling the many virtues and unqualified benefits likely to result from the implementation of their principles.

Looking more closely at this issue, it would seem that behavioralists have vastly oversimplified the entire motivation process and engaged in excessive generalization. Hence, their claims to the *universality* of their findings and the general applicability of their recommendations for the management of human resources must be seriously questioned.

To a great extent, it would appear that many behavioral scientists have lost sight of the tremendous variability that exists among people. They seem to have forgotten one of the psychologists' own basic tenets—the Law of Individual Differences. This fundamental psychological principle tells us that essentially people are not alike. They vary significantly in their psychological needs, motivational patterns, and value systems as they also do in their abilities, personality characteristics, and levels of mental ability. To accept the motivationalists' overgeneralizations about their findings, which are often based on relatively small statistical samples, is to lose sight of reality and the broad context of the actual world of work.

People's Opinion of the Importance of Work Varies

For many employees—and as we shall see shortly in this chapter, not necessarily at only the lower organizational levels—work is simply *not* the most important part of their lives. It may indeed not even be particularly significant. Since the job provides an individual's income, it often serves predominantly as a means to an end—that end frequently being off-the-job leisure or family activities. Of course, this does not mean that employees do not want jobs that are pleasant, interesting, and generally agreeable—clearly all subjective terms whose meaning will vary with each individual. However, many people do not necessarily seek or even expect personal fulfillment through their jobs. Nor are they invariably dissatisfied with their employment, as many behavioral scientists and journalists have reported repeatedly in recent years.

Some observers have gone so far as to claim that there really is no basic job discontent in the first place, and that reports of its supposed existence have been wildly exaggerated, mainly by some social scientists and journalists who have climbed on the bandwagon. Essentially, people's values systems vary significantly. While it is true that some individuals place great emphasis on satisfaction achieved through work, others believe that time to pursue hobbies and personal interests is far more important. As one employee told me some time ago: "I get my kicks off the job." Different strokes for different folks.

People's Need for Job Autonomy and Participation Varies

Motivationalists have consistently stressed the importance that employees place on freedom, independence, and personal autonomy on the job. They have also stressed people's strong need to plan, organize, and control their work and to have a greater participative input in matters directly affecting them. Indeed, emphasis on these factors is the very cornerstone of the work redesign movement. Again, we must ask how universal these employee desires really are.

To answer this question, we must first recognize that people run the gamut with respect to their desire and ability to plan, organize, and control their work. Certainly job autonomy and participation arc important to *some* employees, but this can hardly be called a universal need. As every manager has learned from firsthand experience, not everyone has the intelligence, knowledge, and experience—or the desire—to engage in such work functions. To expect *all* employees to assume such responsibilities—in essence, to foist employee participation upon them—is to risk severe operational difficulties, if not utter work chaos.

In addition, people vary tremendously in their need for job structure. Some employees require a highly structured, clearly defined, and unambiguous work environment where the supervisor provides them with precise instructions about how the job is to be carried out and exactly what is expected of them. Indeed, many people with strong security needs find such a job atmosphere psychologically supportive and report that they perform at their best under these conditions. Exposing such individuals to jobs with considerable autonomy where they must make decisions and participate in more traditional managerial functions would very likely cause them to feel emotionally threatened and experience considerable anxiety, probably leading to ineffectiveness in their work.

At the same time, as many managers have also learned, other employees *do* prefer a relatively loosely structured work environment which provides them with more on-the-job autonomy. These people clearly welcome the opportunity to put their own ideas into practice and enjoy the participative aspects of the job. Even more importantly, under the right circumstances, such individuals frequently can and do make worthwhile contributions to their companies.

Finally, for employees to be capable of participating with management in decision making, they must first identify with the goals and objectives of their organizations. In essence, they must care about their companies. This consideration touches on the entire issue of employee attitude, which we shall discuss later in this chapter. Once again, however, it must be pointed out that employees vary in their identification with their companies. All factors being equal, the more people care about their organization and its problems and goals, the more likely they are to propose positive suggestions for the company's improvement. On the other hand, where employee attitude is more of the I-don't-give-a-damn type, worthwhile employee contributions are not so apt to be forthcoming.

People's Need for Money Varies

In discussing how to motivate employees toward better productivity, behavioral scientists have generally tended to de-emphasize the importance of money. If anything, they have demeaned and deprecated the incentive value of money. Readers will readily recall that Herzberg classified money as a dissatisfier, or hygiene factor, incapable of motivating employees toward improved performance. In fact, the one aspect of current motivational thinking that probably has generated the greaest amount of controversy, as well as considerable skepticism, is the low value that most behavioral scientists have attributed to money. The point is not without its ironic side. Several years ago, in planning a business conference, I approached a well-known authority on motivation to ask that he give a talk on nonfinancial incentives for improving productivity. We were unable to get together, though, because of the excessively high fee he demanded to participate in the conference!

Evaluating the significance of money and financial incentives in general is never simple. Various factors must be considered, for money serves several basic functions. Obviously, it permits us to buy the material goods and services we desire. But money also has a fundamental symbolic and psychological value. A number of years ago, I had a client who was president of a major corporation. His name appeared year after year in business magazines as one of the nation's most highly paid executives. One year, he missed the list and felt rather miffed. When I asked him what difference his not appearing on the list really made, especially in view of his total income and his many other assets, he sheepishly replied: "Well, it's kind of nice to be up there." To a great extent, then, money represents an evaluation of what a person is worth in the eyes of others. The higher our incomes, presumably the greater our value to our organizations.

It is not the objective of this book to discuss the use of financial incentives to motivate people. Many excellent books deal with that subject. Suffice it to say, however, that money does serve a most useful function and does motivate most people, at least to some extent, particularly in view of the horrendous inflation we have experienced and notwithstanding the almost confiscatory income taxes. That money does not motivate some people some of the time, or that some people might say they would not take a particular position no matter what it paid, is really begging the question. Money remains a vital factor in stimulating individual performance, despite the many situational factors that might lessen its significance as an incentive.

Why Are the Behavioralists' Motivational Theories Contradicted by the Evidence?

How can we explain the apparent discrepancy between the motivational theories of the behavioral science "greats" and some of the contradictory evidence presented in this chapter about individual variations in work motivation? To what can we attribute the overgeneralization and oversimplification with which the motivational school has espoused its findings? I think the answer can best be found by looking at the people who formulated the motivational concepts. We have already pointed out that the behavioral scientists were influenced by strong humanistic values. This orientation no doubt caused them to overidealize individual employees and ascribe to them all sorts of latent talents, abilities, and potential contributions that industrial-organizational psychologists felt were simply waiting to be brought out on behalf of organizational problem solving. The preceding pages have already suggested that this is an overly optimistic and somewhat unrealistic expectation that in many instances is unlikely to materialize. We cannot actually expect *all* employees to have such lofty qualifications as behavioral scientists would have us believe.

Going a bit further, motivationalists have in effect fallen into their own trap by succumbing to the very common psychological reaction known as projection. Placing great value themselves on achieving self-fulfillment and recognizing their own strong need for independence and autonomy in their work, they have projected these same needs upon others and accordingly have attributed their own motivation to the general population.

Indeed, the behavioral scientists whose work we have reviewed were basically academicians, firmly steeped in university traditions. As such, a major attribute of their life styles as college professors is that they experience considerable personal fulfillment as well as maximum autonomy in their work. Because these behavioral scientists have spent most of their lives in this type of academic environment, they appear to have drawn a most natural conclusion, assuming that since independence and autonomy are so important to them, they invariably must be equally important to the general population. The foregoing factors, I believe, may explain the discrepancy between currently popular motivational concepts and some of the findings we have pointed out.

Changing Attitudes Toward Work

One of the major factors contributing to the variability and frequent decline currently seen in employee motivation is that many people have undergone a profound change in their attitudes toward work. Historically, Americans have been taught that success comes from working hard and putting their shoulders firmly to the wheel. Indeed, the work ethic has long been an integral part of the American way of life and our cultural heritage. The belief that personal diligence and application will pay off in the end has always been stressed in the home, at schools and colleges, and by our religious institutions.

Then again, the necessity of working hard also had, at least to some extent, a basis in fear—the fear of being out of work and possibly facing dire consequences. Some older Americans may still remember the Great Depression of the 1930s and the widespread hardships it caused. But this memory, which was based on fear as a motivating factor and which at one time might have spurred people to work more diligently, is fading rapidly for the vast majority of people. Particularly for today's younger population, this memory has little relevance whatsoever.

This is not to say that the work ethic is entirely dead—although in some places it may very well be ailing—or that willingness to work hard and fully apply oneself to the requirements of a job no longer exists. Nevertheless, there is a good deal of evidence, both anecdotal as well as from systematic research, to indicate that the work ethic is not as healthy as it once was. Many people simply do not want to work too hard any longer, or put another way, we shall see that the will to work varies considerably from person to person.

In this regard, Daniel Yankelovich, the prominent public opinion pollster who probably has surveyed more people about their attitudes toward work than anyone else, has uncovered some rather disturbing data. For example, in questioning college students about whether "hard work always pays off," respondents answered yes 70 percent of the time in 1967. However, by 1973, the number of students replying in the affirmative had dropped significantly to 40 percent. Furthermore, in the late 1960s, slightly less than half of all employed Americans looked to their jobs as a source of personal fulfillment; by 1980, the figure had fallen to less than one out of four. Indeed, Yankelovich reports that better than four out of five of all working people regard their leisure-time activities as more important than their work.

This is not to say that there aren't many people who are ambitious, motivated, and eager to get ahead. However, Yankelovich points out emphatically, and backed by substantial empirical evidence, that a large group of people simply are no longer motivated to work as hard or as effectively as in the past. In fact, he goes so far as to state that some 27 percent of the work force are essentially turned off by their jobs, and he fears that this group is very likely to be the cause of future social unrest.*

In recent years, there have been numerous reports that many of our young college and university graduates simply are not of the caliber that they used to be—that they are not willing to work as hard as were previous generations. While many have scoffed at such observations, recent data reported by AT&T throw new and rather alarming light on this subject.

In their well-known longitudinal studies of managers within the Bell System, Ann Howard and Douglas W. Bray, two highly respected researchers, have in fact documented some very significant motivational differences between managers hired in the mid-1950s and those who joined the

* Daniel Yankelovich, "We Need New Motivational Tools," *Industry Week*, August 6, 1979, pp. 61–68.

telephone company some 20 years later.* While the researchers found no differences between the two groups in average *ability* level, they did find the current generation of managers to be less upward aspiring in their desire for advancement than had been true of the earlier generation. Howard and Bray believe the data they have obtained accurately reflect the attitudes and values, not only of younger managers within the Bell System, but also of the country's younger managers in general. As a result, they express concern about how American business and industry will be able to find the necessary leaders in sufficient numbers to manage our organizations in the future.

Nor were Howard and Bray's AT&T findings limited only to younger Bell System managers. Their continuing "Management Progress Study" dealing with the lives and careers of telephone company managers hired over many years indicated that, in general, the expectation and desire for job advancement is not all that strong. Interestingly, in contrast with Herzberg's concepts, many Bell System managers indicated a reluctance to accept the additional responsibility that higher-level management assignments would entail, implying that jobs were becoming less important in the managers' lives than family or recreational activities.†

One does not have to be a skilled researcher and generate volumes of detailed empirical evidence to conclude that many people simply do not want to put out as much effort as in the past. Many managers and executives have made the same observation from personal experience. For

* Ann Howard and Douglas W. Bray, "Continuities and Discontinuities between Two Generations of Bell System Managers," paper presented at the American Psychological Association Annual Convention, Montreal, Canada, September 1980.
† Ann Howard and Douglas W. Bray, "Career Motivation in Mid-Life Managers," paper presented at the American Psychological Association Annual Convention, Montreal, Canada, September 1980.

example, the sales vice president of a major *Fortune* 500 industrial manufacturing corporation with a generally good track record in personnel selection recently told me the following story.

His company was enjoying considerable sales success, brought about mainly by a particularly strong market demand for its technologically superior line of products. In fact, the organization's production facilities were operating nearly at maximum capacity, and present output was just about sold up. Nevertheless, at a weekly meeting with the sales force, the company's sales vice president emphasized that, even though business was currently going extremely well, it was imiortant to look ahead and plan for the future. He stressed the need to improve and build upon the company's customer relations, not just for today, but more significantly for tomorrow. In this connection, he urged his people, many of them generally younger, to get out of the sales office more often, to keep on making customer calls, and to visit their accounts. To his amazement, many of these employees responded angrily, saying that they had already met their sales quotas and were therefore entitled to stay around the office and take it a little easy. They further indicated they strongly resented what they regarded as the sales manager's imposing upon them. They felt he was hounding them and believed that, having sold their immediate quotas, they had earned the right to sit back and relax a bit.

What has brought about this change in so many people's attitudes toward work? Once again, social scientists offer numerous hypotheses. I would personally volunteer four very likely explanations (although the lines separating them might at times be a bit indistinct): the affluence of recent years, a prevailing psychology of entitlement, an increase in self-indulgence on the part of many, and finally, a decline in work application by some people.

Affluence of Recent Years

One of the reasons for changing work attitudes may very well be the relative affluence the nation has enjoyed for many years. While it is true that the country has experienced several economic peaks and valleys over the years, the United States has essentially enjoyed unprecedented prosperity since the end of World War II. Consequently, the fear of losing one's job and not readily finding another—of being totally unable to support oneself and one's family—has become less and less a concern for an increasing number of people. While fear of unemployment and the resulting economic hardships might well have historically been a motivating factor that kept people's noses to the grindstone, losing one's job is much less of a personal crisis today.

Furthermore, as we shall see in a later section of this chapter, various government support programs, most notably unemployment insurance, have significantly softened the blow of being out of work. Moreover, while in the past the male head of a household might have felt somewhat less of a man being unemployed, this is no longer a common perception. With the vast increase in the number of working wives, the spouse's income is very likely to tide the family over quite nicely until the husband regains employment in a labor market that over the years has risen to the very respectable current figure of nearly 100 million jobs.

To digress for a moment, Clark Kerr, Chairman of the Board of Directors of The Work in America Institute and President Emeritus of the University of California, has made a philosophical point worth considering. He feels the very act of working hard may eventually bring on a decline in the will to work itself, saying "There are inherent contradictions between emerging life-styles and old-fashioned attitudes toward work. The work ethic in the longer run may yet turn out to contain within itself the 'seeds of its own destruction': hard work leads to affluence; affluence leads to new life-styles; new life-styles diminish the work ethic." * The question for the nation may well be what steps need to be taken to enable us to enjoy a full and satisfying life while maintaining our economic viability.

Psychology of Entitlement

Very closely linked to the changing attitudes toward work, which are attributable to the relative prosperity the nation has generally enjoyed for the past several decades, is the emergence of what is currently referred to as the "psychology of entitlement." To describe this psychology succinctly: Many people nowadays feel that they have coming to them—in essence, that they deserve—certain benefits, privileges, and rights merely by virtue of living in today's world. Put another way, these individuals believe very strongly that society owes them a comfortable economic base, in the form of various material conditions, as a minimum guarantee from which they can expect to proceed. As such, they feel they have a basic right to enjoy the satisfaction of certain conditions without necessarily having had to expend a lot of effort to obtain them in the first place. Some social scientists have pointed out that this attitude, which prevails among many people and which numerous critics find quite objectionable, is a direct outgrowth of our permissive and affluent society.

How is this expectation of entitlement expressed? We often find it initially in the home, where children, having seen the tangible results of their parents' hard work and consistent diligence over the course of the many years of their careers, now demand the use of the family car or credit card or other material objects as an *entitlement,* to which they feel they have an automatic right. We see it also

* Clark Kerr and Jerome M. Rosow, *Work in America: The Decade Ahead* (New York: Van Nostrand Reinhold, 1979), p. xx.

in high schools and universities, where students voice the expectation that they are *entitled* to good grades without having to push themselves all that hard. In fact, in my contacts with graduate students, many have told me outright that they felt they practically deserved a minimum grade of B, because, after all, they had enrolled in the course I was teaching.

Perhaps most noticeably, we find the psychology of entitlement quite prevalent among many employees who feel they have virtually a guaranteed right to a "good" job. A large group of our current college graduates believe they are entitled to a desirable job, if for no other reason than they put in a certain number of years in college and now, as a reward, are due a good job with, of course, the level of salary which will enable them to enjoy the material comforts of the "good life." A number of years ago, then as a personnel executive, I was involved in college recruiting and visited numerous campuses. It was not all that unusual for a nonchalant student to sit back during the course of the interview and ask matter-of-factly: "What does *your* company have to offer *me?*"

Probably the worst manifestation of this attitude of being entitled to desirable work comes to light when out-of-work employees—customarily drawing unemployment insurance and possibly collecting welfare or food stamps—outright refuse jobs for which they are qualified only because, in their judgment, they are not "good" jobs. Even during periods of relatively high unemployment, we increasingly find the paradoxical phenomenon of a substantial number of people being out of work, while simultaneously a substantial number of job vacancies go begging because people view them as "bad" or undesirable jobs. In this connection, it is commonly reported that many of the nation's low-level, unskilled jobs—for example, those in the restaurant, hotel, and many service industries—would remain unfilled if it were not for the illegal immigrants.

They enter the country and are willing to take these openings, while so many of our *own* citizens simply will not.

In a related vein, while working as a personnel executive some years ago, I well recall a number of employees voluntarily resigning from their jobs and going to Florida for an extra vacation, while simultaneously drawing unemployment insurance. These people felt they were entitled to a subsidized vacation, and despite the fact that the unemployment insurance authorities were notified that these individuals had voluntarily left their jobs and accordingly had no right to unemployment compensation, they nevertheless were granted the insurance payments. (The fact that many people are thus abusing and circumventing both the spirit and the letter of unemployment insurance laws clearly calls for determined corrective action by appropriate government officials.)

Increase in Self-Indulgence

In my opinion, the permissiveness and affluence of recent years has also led to excessive self-indulgence and hedonism on the part of many people, with a resultant decline in their productivity and work performance. It would seem that many individuals emphasize pleasure seeking and instant gratification—in essence, having fun and enjoying themselves to the hilt. While I make no attempt here to propose a return to the Calvinist philosophy, or even necessarily to advocate workaholism, I do think there exists an unhealthy imbalance, with undue emphasis on pleasure-seeking pursuits at the expense of productive activity.

We have heard a great deal about today's "new breed" or "me generation." It has been suggested that these types are the wave of the future, and business will have to accommodate itself to them. One of the main characteristics of this sector of our population is the stress they place on their own gratification, with relatively little consideration for any possible obligation to the rest of society. During the past several years, we have seen the appearance of a number of articles and books, obviously catering to this group, that extol the virtues of being self-centered, looking out for number one, and exhibiting a What's-in-it-for-me? attitude at the expense of self-discipline. To discover a related facet of the problem, one need only look at the increase in drug abuse which has been a serious concern for some time now to many employers. In fact, we are told by some writers in the popular press that it is all right—even emotionally healthy—to "do your own thing" without being too concerned about its possible effect on other people.

Many individuals who are inherently disposed to subscribe to the work ethic must invariably begin to think that perhaps there is something wrong with *them* when they come across excerpts such as the following, which glorify the pursuit of pleasure while demeaning productive work:

> In this country there is an option to working, which is not working. I'm not a believer that intrinsically we want to work. Intrinsically, we want to have a good time. I am convinced that the pursuit of pleasure in this country has become the focus of a lot of people's lives and more and more so . . . my work experience has always given me real doubt about man's intrinsic desire to work. There are increasingly attractive alternatives to hard work and people are learning to use them. Why work hard if we have a choice? *

Similarly, for the first time we hear of not a few women who abandon their children to "find themselves" in activities they feel will be more meaningful and rewarding than childrearing. And amazingly, we even have a recent

---

* Robert Schrank, *Ten Thousand Working Days* (Cambridge, Mass.: MIT Press, 1978).

book filled with some rather specific advice on how to live—and live moderately well—without working. This book, which has sold relatively well, is not aimed at welfare cheats. Rather, it tells employable, middle-class people how they can wheel and deal, use chicanery, and get around rules and regulations in order to sponge off society by becoming eligible for unemployment insurance, welfare, and food stamps! *

I think in general that we have seen a decline in respect for and adherence to established authority and rules and regulations on the part of many people, with a growing preference for behavior that clearly places higher priority on what is personally most rewarding. Note, for example, the alarming trend toward violating traffic regulations, illustrated by such examples as speeding and going through red lights and stop signs. Some social scientists have suggested the decline in respect for the law can be attributed to a general malaise, cynicism, and lack of confidence in our institutions brought about by such events as Vietnam, Watergate, publicized individual and corporate tax evasion, and various political wrongdoings and scandals, such as Abscam. While opinions may differ about the causes, most people will agree that the problem exists and appears to be worsening.

Decline in Work Application

Looking at the productivity problem in perspective, it has become clear to most observers that a large proportion of people from all walks of life simply do not want to work as hard as they did in the past. For all the reasons discussed in this chapter, the result seems to be that many people do not exert themselves all that much any more, nor do they apply themselves as diligently and as conscientiously as has

---

* Bernard Lefkowitz, *Break-Time: Living Without Work in a Nine-to-Five World* (New York: Hawthorne Books, 1979).

historically been the case. Indeed, in the opinion of numerous critics, many people have, as the saying goes, become "fat, lazy, and complacent." Hence, while I would not go so far as to pronounce the work ethic dead, I do not think it too inaccurate to pronounce it ailing and in need of a good dose of revitalization.

Nor is this attitude limited only to the workplace. Educational authorities have reported the same decline in diligence among students for many years, as evidenced, for example, by the dramatic drop in college admissions test scores. In this connection, many students, in high school as well as in college, seem to be opting for the easier courses. And regrettably, our educational institutions are frequently only too accommodating. They make it relatively easy for students to drop the more difficult courses (or those taught by the more demanding instructors); they institute pass-fail grading systems; and they often modify educational requirements, thus effectively lowering academic standards. Is it any wonder, then, that many students, having graduated from such institutions, arrive on the job with inappropriate work attitudes and expectations?

It is incongruous that work application, productivity, and commitment to organizational goals have all declined precisely during a period when compensation, benefits, and many job perquisites have dramatically increased. In 1979, for example, the Labor Department reported that employee compensation and unit labor costs in the United States rose 9 and 11.5 percent respectively, while productivity actually fell by 2 percent, clearly fueling our inflation problem and further damaging our competitive position in the area of international trade. People have basically felt entitled to an ever increasing standard of living and, indeed, have achieved this goal, but so very often they have not put forth the effort, energy, and application needed to generate a corresponding rise in productivity and thereby support the increased income they were receiving.

Amazingly, despite the employee gains cited above, one rarely hears any mention that *employees* have an obligation to the employers. In all their writings, the motivationalists have focused attention on the obligation that the *company* has to its employees. While the idea of the company's obligation is all well and good, and there is no argument on this score, do not employees *also* have an obligation to identify with their companies? In return for the paychecks they draw, do employees not also owe a commitment to the goals and objectives of their employers? Obligation and commitment are, after all, a two-way street, entailing responsibility on the part of both the company and the employees. Perhaps the motivationalists implied all along that such a reciprocity exists. However, it would seem that this point has largely been overlooked and needs to be restated and more clearly emphasized.

Increase in Government Social Support Programs

There can hardly be any doubt that productivity and work application would be considerably greater today were it not for the existence of a host of government social support programs designed to assist the unemployed. Historically, the specter of losing one's job evoked considerable fear and anxiety in most people. Indeed, the prospect of being without work and consequently being unable to support oneself and one's family was a veritable nightmare for many. In all probability, it caused employees to expend considerable effort on behalf of their jobs.

Today such concerns no longer exist, at least not with the same intensity. Americans, and fortunately so, no longer believe that a catastrophe will result if they lose their jobs. A problem, perhaps; a minor crisis, maybe; but a dire tragedy, no. Indeed, we have in our country today an array of government social support programs which help people in time of need. Unemployment insurance compensation is readily available, and during periods of serious economic downturn or prolonged recession, the benefits are usually liberalized and the length of time recipients can claim payments is continually extended.

It is in fact commonly known that workers who are laid off frequently enjoy a higher income when they are out of work than they customarily earned on their regular jobs. This is because they often earn unreported income doing odd jobs around their neighborhoods, and this income, combined with unemployment insurance and possibly any supplementary unemployment benefits to which they are entitled, plus their savings in transportation and lunch expenses causes them to be better off *un*employed than employed.

Moreover, government support programs are not limited to unemployment insurance compensation. Food stamps are customarily readily available to those out of work, and numerous other assistance programs exist for those who find themselves in need. In short, the crisis aspect as such has been removed from unemployment.

It should be stressed that in no way am I advocating the abolition of such essential government social support programs. I strongly feel, though, that, in many instances, they are in dire need of substantial administrative improvement. While it is not the purpose of this book to offer a detailed blueprint for improving such programs, I do think, as mentioned earlier, that it is basically improper, totally unacceptable, and a distortion of the law for workers to continue receiving unemployment insurance when they have removed themselves voluntarily from the job market and are merely taking an extra vacation. I would make a similar point about employees who turn down "bad" jobs for which they are qualified simply because they feel themselves entitled to "better" jobs. (While on this topic, in my opinion there is no such thing as a "bad" job, if it permits an individual to earn a wage in keeping with his or her qualifications. Rather, as I see it, there are jobs and there are better jobs. People should take the best jobs they can get and stay with them until they are able to work their way up to better positions.)

The following story, recently told to me by an executive, aptly illustrates the extent to which the fear, embarrassment, and even shame that might at one time have been associated with being out of work no longer exist. The executive found it necessary to discharge a secretary for unsatisfactory work and excessive lateness. Moreover, having been brought up during the Great Depression of the 1930s, when being out of work was a veritable personal disaster, he felt and acted quite regretful, sympathetic, and even a bit apologetic in dismissing his secretary. For her part, however, the secretary felt no such emotions and, in fact, became notably supportive of the man firing her, saying, "Oh, don't feel so badly about this, Mr. Taylor. It's no big deal to get fired: I'll get another job without any trouble." In short, while government social support programs have very likely enhanced people's feelings of security, in so doing they may also have helped foster certain negative work attitudes.

Summary

To recapitulate, in the first chapter, we examined the problem of declining productivity growth and the threat it poses to our country's posture in the world, our continued high standard of living, and the very way of life to which Americans have become accustomed over the years. In the following chapter, we explored the most prevalent and widely accepted of the current theories about employee behavior and work motivation, which according to the experts, would virtually guarantee a never-ending increase in productivity. And in the present chapter, we have seen that things do not always work out as theorists anticipate: We were forced to confront the uncomfortable realization that many employees simply are not motivated to put forth their best efforts on behalf of their jobs.

Yet clearly our organizations' work needs to be done, particularly if the goals and objectives of our companies and of our nation are to be met. Given the diversity and variability of employee values, attitudes, and work motivation, how then are managers to best direct their people so that satisfactory levels of productivity will be attained? This issue will be the focus of the next chapter.

4
Reality-Centered Management

❧

The Key to
Organizational Effectiveness

Countless books and articles have been written over the years advising managers how best to supervise their people in order to improve productivity. The recommendations offered have ranged from relatively simple, almost homespun solutions, more or less based on common sense, and approaches advocating the golden rule to calls for fairly complex and sophisticated managerial behavior strategies. At varying times, we have been told to "be fair but firm," to adopt a democratic leadership style, or to engage in participative management practices, to name only a few such seemingly helpful proposals. In fact, hardly a month passes that managers do not find in their in-baskets some article urging them to adopt a particular leadership style or approach as the elusive key to better managing their people. This issue currently has taken on increased urgency in view of the nation's concern with strategies for increasing productivity.

In the closing decades of the twentieth century, America's attention will undoubtedly focus primarily on ways to increase the nation's productivity. The watchword everywhere is industrialization, and there are many calls for what is varyingly termed the "revitalization" or "regeneration" of America's economic resources and for a "second industrial revolution." It is important to recognize that declining productivity growth and its consequences is clearly a multidimensional problem. Hence, numerous coordinated approaches will be needed if we are to effectively attack and overcome it. Certainly no one solution can entirely restore productivity to the desired level.

We have already suggested in Chapter 1 that such a combined effort will be necessary, and that it must include, among other steps, strategies to increase our nation's expenditures on research and development, fiscal and tax policies to encourage massive investment in new capital equipment and technology, and specific ways to reduce the cost and burden of excessive government regulations. In addition, however, dynamic and more workable strategies must also be found to more effectively manage our nation's human resources. This will be the thrust of the present chapter.

Managers have gotten a good deal of advice in recent years on how to direct their employees for better productivity. The prevailing message has basically been that the overwhelming majority of people have a strong, almost inherent, need to achieve personal fulfillment through their jobs. It is said that the way for people to find fulfillment and simultaneously for companies to best utilize their human resources to attain increased productivity is to enhance jobs and permit employees to participate extensively in management decision making.

The previous chapter has illustrated, however, that this is a very broad generalization. It may be quite idealistic and humanistic, but it is also in many ways not particularly realistic. This sweeping assumption about human behavior on the job is simply not categorically supported by the facts. Realistically speaking, many people do not really seek the basic satisfaction in their lives through work, nor are they actually capable of or even interested in engaging in joint decision making with management, despite what behavioralists so staunchly claim.

To many people, the job is basically a means to an end—the end very likely being satisfaction gained through their leisure-time activities. This is not to say that there are not numerous people who *are* notably challenged and stimulated by their work, and who *are* strongly interested in having a greater impact on what goes on in their departments. But it is misleading to suggest that joint decision making is a *universal* need of all workers.

As we have seen, people essentially are very different from one another, and a tremendous variability exists among the employees in any organization. To some, the job is very important, and they are strongly motivated by their work; to others, work has a far lower priority. Similarly, some have a rather intense need to participate in matters directly affecting their employment, while others are quite content, indeed eager, to have management make these decisions for them. Hence, it is unrealistic and grossly misleading to overgeneralize and attribute a single set of qualities to *all* employees. Nor is it in any way a useful strategy for social scientists and journalists to go on a crusade, urging managers to encourage all their employees to engage in joint decision making with them.

In the same way that people differ from each other, so do organizations. Certainly the problems, conditions, and challenges faced by a research laboratory staffed by highly experienced scientific and technical professionals can be expected to differ substantially from those of a manufacturing company staffed predominantly by semiskilled or unskilled labor. While the employees of the research laboratory might very well be seeking maximum fulfillment on the job and would very likely respond excellently to a highly participative leadership style, such an approach would probably be disastrous if blindly and dogmatically applied to employees in the manufacturing plant.

Looking at the actual world of work in a more realistic fashion, one readily realizes that there exist many relatively standardized, highly structured, and fairly repetitive jobs. They nevertheless serve a useful purpose and clearly need to be done. But who is to say that such work is intrinsically boring or monotonous? Perhaps to a behavioral scientist or a journalist highly standardized and repetitive production jobs might be intolerable. However, this must not necessarily be assumed to be the case with all persons actually performing such work. Monotony and boredom in the final analysis are in the eyes of the beholder. Indeed, the type of work that might stimulate and challenge a behavioral scientist would very likely be viewed quite negatively by a person on the production line. Again, very different people often have very different needs.

In fact, as we have seen in the last chapter, many people *do* prefer moderately standardized, repetitive, and structured types of jobs that they feel they can handle comfortably and that do not make too many demands on them. These workers are perfectly happy and willing to have management make the necessary on-the-job decisions for them, and in fact, many would probably suffer a certain amount of tension and anxiety should management thrust them into a participative role for which they feel unprepared.

Nor is there anything inherently wrong or undesirable in such standardized, repetitive, and structured jobs, as some writers have claimed. In the first place, not every work function can be redesigned or enhanced in the way job enrichment supporters would have management believe. Numerous technological, financial, and administrative barriers actually prevent many jobs from ever being substantially enriched. But beyond that, many jobs which must necessarily be highly structured and standardized nevertheless often provide very essential services. Some examples would be the many relatively low-level jobs in hospitals, nursing homes, or restaurants, to name only a few settings. While such work might be somewhat uninspiring and understandably rather unappealing to many people, this is not to say that others do not regard this type of employment as more than acceptable. Frequently they welcome the stability and steady income that such positions provide. Nor am I ready to accept the blanket condemnation of an attendant's job in a senior citizens' facility—to pick just one illustration—as work that is "bad" or demeaning per se. As I see it, no jobs are "bad" jobs if they serve a needed purpose.

In essence, then, many very different types of jobs exist in many very different types of organizations. These jobs call for a wide variety of abilities, interests, and talents and accordingly make very different demands on the people holding them. Fortunately, as we have observed, there also exists a comparably wide diversity among employees. Hence, a given person may be ill suited to a specific position in one company, but clearly well suited to another job in a different organization.

Effective management therefore calls for a realistic appraisal of what type of individual is right for a given assignment and under what type of supervision and direction. As such, there is no *one* style of leadership that will fit all employees and be appropriate in all organizations under all circumstances. Sam Zagoria, then Director of the Labor-Management Relations Service of the U.S. Conference of Mayors, best summed up this point in a recent speech, when he said:

All workers are not alike; they are not cast from the same mold. They come in assorted shapes, sizes, education and experience, attitudes and ambitions. Some work for a living; for others working is living. Some think of work as their central purpose in life; others consider work as a way of providing the necessities and look to the time away from work as the real joy of living. The net of this is that while many workers look on their jobs as unexciting, boring, repetitive exercises that require only part of their potential capability, others enjoy the regularity, repetition, and steadiness of a job. They are delighted to leave to a management all the headaches and heartaches of a competitive, high-risk economy. Truly, one man's straitjacket may be another's security blanket.*

Reality-Centered Management

If organizations are to more effectively use their human resources, I believe we must adopt a different approach to managing people than what has been urged upon us in the past. I do not favor dogmatically following any single leadership style and attempting to apply it rigidly to all people and to all situations. Instead, what I feel is called for is a flexible approach to managing employees—an approach that realistically reflects the specific conditions, factors, and circumstances that actually exist in the total work environment in which managers function. Hence, the term *Reality-Centered Management.*

This approach to managing people fully takes into account the type of employees being supervised, particularly recognizing their differing abilities and diverse motivational needs, as well as all relevant factors existing in

* Reprinted with permission.

the specific organization. This approach recognizes that managers will always have some people reporting to them who want to express themselves, who seek maximum personal fulfillment through their work, and who, as a result, may be quite eager to participate with management in decision-making activities. At the same time, however, managers will always have on their staffs certain other individuals who do not place the same importance on work, and who consequently look to managers for clear and explicit direction and supportive supervision. As such, effective managers will need a flexible leadership style which will enable them to utilize a participative approach with some employees, while adopting a much more directive and supportive posture with other employees, depending on the style that is more appropriate to the employees' individual needs and abilities.

Reality-Centered Management regards leadership style as a continuum, ranging from highly directive management to a notably more participative approach. It should not be viewed as a dichotomous model, however. Each manager's own natural leadership style and manner of supervising employees will tend to favor either a directive or a participative approach, but it is most unlikely that any manager's style will fall exclusively at either extreme of the continuum.

The point I wish to emphasize is that, while managers have their inherent preferences in leadership styles, effective managers need to be *flexible* in their approach to managing people. They must possess the ability to adapt their leadership style appropriately in response to the individual characteristics of particular employees and the unique requirements and conditions of specific situations. Therefore, the next two sections will help you better understand the management approach you have typically been using and present some strategies for selecting an appropriate management approach.

What Is Your Customary Management Style?

Research has shown that all managers have a preferred leadership style that they customarily follow. This management approach usually evolves over several years and is formed gradually as a result of the subtle interplay of various factors, particularly the actual experience the managers have gained in supervising personnel and the type of leadership style with which they are personally most comfortable.

As might be anticipated, managers differ substantially with respect to t e type of leadership they think they should exercise with their people. Some believe they should demonstrate strong personal leadership and place considerable value on making decisions and providing structure for their employees. Others lean toward the participative side and place considerable value on allowing their employees to help make decisions about matters directly affecting them.

Then again managers must, of necessity, be influenced by their own assessment of the competence of their staff to engage in joint decision making. Clearly, managers who have found in the past that their people responded favorably to participative management, and especially if their employees offered some useful suggestions which had a positive effect, will tend to favor a more participative approach. The opposite will be the case where managers have tried the participative approach with unsatisfactory results or feel their subordinates lack the basic competence to engage in joint decision making.

To find out what your *own* customary management style is, please take a few moments right now to complete and score the Management Style Questionnaire which appears at the end of this chapter. In answering the questionnaire, bear in mind that it is not a test, nor are there any "right" or "wrong" responses, and that to gain maximum insight into your management style it is essential that your responses reflect your own most typical attitudes and behaviors.

Having completed the Management Style Questionnaire, your logical question is, "What does my score mean?" The range of possible total scores is from 30 to 120 points. The lower your score, the more directive your typical management style is apt to be. Conversely, the higher your score, the more likely you are to customarily exercise a more participative leadership approach. It should be emphasized that the score is purely descriptive, not evaluative: There is no "good" or "bad" score. The important consideration, as we shall see in the following section, is that managers develop both the ability to accurately evaluate managerial situations in which they find themselves and the flexibility to utilize the leadership style which is most appropriate for the particular situation.

Selecting the Right Management Approach

Now that you have taken the Management Style Questionnaire, how do you know whether you are using the right management style to fit the total needs of your particular situation? To respond to this very strategic question, let us take a look at some of the factors that would suggest that a manager's style should lean either toward the directive or the participative end of the continuum.

Factors Suggesting a More Directive Management Style

Employees tend to be more leisure oriented, rather than seeking to fulfill themselves through the job.

Employees' job experience is such that they lack the requisite qualifications to take on greater responsibilities.

Employees' educational or skill levels are relatively modest.

Employees have a personal reluctance to take on additional job responsibilities.

Employees require a relatively structured, clearly defined, and essentially unambiguous work environment in order to perform most effectively.

Employees need fairly close and supportive supervision.

Employees do not express a personal interest in becoming involved in decision-making activities.

Employees fail to identify strongly with the goals and objectives of the organization.

FACTORS SUGGESTING A MORE PARTICIPATIVE MANAGEMENT STYLE

Employees seek fulfillment of many of their ego and psychological needs through the job.

Employees have the necessary intelligence, education, and experience to take on additional responsibilities.

Employees are interested in having a greater say in matters affecting them on the job and want to engage in decision making with management.

Employees have sufficient tolerance for and receptivity to ambiguity and do not feel anxious, uncomfortable, or insecure when faced with relatively unstructured and loosely defined work situations.

Employees are self-reliant and self-confident and do not need close and supportive supervision.

Employees identify strongly with the goals and objectives of the organization.

After examining the factors listed above which would suggest a more directive or a more participative management style, you may find it extremely helpful to compare them with the characteristics of your *own* present management situation. Do the unique realities of the situation you confront appear to call for a more directive or a more participative management style? Then consider the insight you gained about your typical managerial approach from the Management Style Questionnaire. Are you in fact utilizing the approach that is best suited to the actual needs of your management situation? If there appears to be a discrepancy between the recommended style and your customary style, you might wish to begin developing some strategies to change your management approach to better respond to the realities of the situation in which you are operating.

Now let us consider two case studies which illustrate how the factors suggesting a more participative or a more directive management style are applied in typical work situations.

WHERE DIRECTIVE MANAGEMENT WORKS BEST
CASE OF DOLORES FLEMING, ADMINISTRATIVE ASSISTANT

Dolores Fleming has been an administrative assistant to Jim Brewer, a senior buyer in the purchasing department of Associated Metals, for the past three years. She was originally hired as a senior secretary to the same buyer five years ago. When her superior moved up in the department two years later, her job started to involve somewhat greater responsibility and a heavier workload, resulting in her promotion to administrative assistant.

Ms. Fleming, who is 48 years old, is married and has three children: two married daughters who have moved away and a son currently completing high school. She is from a large midwestern city and, after her high school graduation, attended business school. She held several secretarial jobs in the downtown business area before leaving work to raise her family. Mr. Fleming works for the city as a police sergeant. Five years ago, with her children no longer so dependent on her, Ms. Fleming had started to get somewhat restless at home. This, together with the fact that with inflation the extra money would come in handy, prompted Ms. Fleming to return to work. At that point, she joined Associated Metals.

Ms. Fleming is of average intelligence. Although somewhat shy and introverted, except when she is with close friends and relatives, she is a most pleasant and unassuming person. Most important, her technical skills are truly superb; they are unquestionably her strong point. She can take rapid shorthand, and her letters and reports are invariably impeccably typed. She enjoys her job with Associated Metals and feels that she has been well treated by the company. In this regard, she thinks she is fairly paid, having gotten periodic salary increases, and believes the company benefits are a least equal to, if not perhaps a bit better than, those of other companies in the city.

But most important, Ms. Fleming enjoys working for Jim Brewer. She has described him as a fine and thoughtful person who does not make unreasonable demands on her, and who treats her with courtesy and consideration. In return, she does her very best to help him in any way she can, often staying late to finish a report or an assignment and, in general, giving the job that little extra that so often makes the difference.

In describing Dolores Fleming and her work performance, her superior, Jim Brewer, is most complimentary: "Dolores has done a super job here and has been of great help to me for the past five years. She has really gotten to know me and how I like to work, and I value her excellent stenographic skills. Is she a *perfect* employee? Well, I doubt that, but then who is?

"Dolores needs to be told exactly what has to be done, precisely how the job is to be handled, and what specific difficulties or problems to be on the lookout for. She is somewhat fearful of making a mistake and really has very little creativity, drive, or initiative. Since she is somewhat shy with others, some people who tend to be more on the assertive side have at times taken advantage of her. However, as long as I tell her exactly what I want done, she will do it to the best of her ability. I just have to be around if she has a problem. However, her attitude, willingness, and cooperation can't be beat. I wish everybody were like Dolores!

"We considered moving Dolores up and training her as a junior purchasing agent as part of our company's affirmative action program, but she wasn't really interested in taking the job. She said she thought there would be too much pressure in the assignment, she really did not want the added responsibility, and she felt she would not be very good at negotiating prices and terms with our vendors. And I must say I agreed with her.

"Dolores probably works best under fairly close supervision, where she knows exactly what to do and can follow precise instructions. She tends to get confused, rattled, and kind of uncomfortable when unexpected problems come up. But you see, we have other people around to take care of those situations. Dolores is a good administrative assistant, and I know what she can do and what her limitations are. I don't ask her to take on assignments that she can't handle. But her secretarial skills and her overall attitude—I wish we had more like her."

Where Participative Management Works Best
Case of Steve Rollins, Assistant Credit Manager

Steve Rollins has been assistant credit manager at the Consolidated Paper Company for the past three years. He is 28 years old, married, and the father of two young children. Rollins earned his B.S. in finance at the State University and is currently enrolled in its business school's M.B.A.

program downtown, where he attends classes two evenings a week. His major is management.

Rollins worked his way through college by driving cabs and tending bars approximately 20 hours a week. Following graduation, he joined Dun & Bradstreet as a credit analyst. Here he checked, analyzed, and evaluated the credit standing of commercial accounts and wrote reports. Toward the end of his stay with the company, he was promoted to assistant supervisor for his unit. Rollins remained with Dun & Bradstreet for three years, resigning when he saw a newspaper advertisement for what appeared to him to be a better job with his present company.

Tom Whiting, credit manager and Rollins' boss at Consolidated Paper, describes him as follows: "Steve is an excellent man. I have been here now going on 18 years, and Steve is among the better people I have had in this assignment. He's bright, ambitious, hard working, and very eager to learn. In addition, Steve can really take hold of an assignment and see it through to completion. He doesn't need me to head him in the right direction or hold his hand. That doesn't mean I'm not here when he runs into trouble and needs help. However, he has the knack of digging into a problem, finding out what caused the difficulty, and coming up with a workable solution. What I'm saying is that he is quite a self-starter with a lot of drive and initiative.

"For example, I recently gave Steve the assignment of seeing how we might be able to speed up collections from some of our larger paper jobbers who were starting to systematically fall behind in meeting agreed-upon credit terms. He really studied that situation thoroughly, went out into the field and talked with credit people in allied industries, and came back with a new program which we have since successfully implemented without in any way upsetting good customer relations with those accounts. At the same time, it has speeded up our cash flow considerably.

"I've been able to turn over a lot of assignments to Steve, which has freed me, in turn, to take on special projects from my boss, the treasurer. Steve is a real go-getter who will surely move ahead. I would have no hesitation in recommending him for my job should I move up in the company."

Putting Reality-Centered Management to Work

As this chapter has emphasized, people differ tremendously in the importance that work plays in their lives. To some, the job is indeed paramount: It may, in fact, be the focal point of their entire existence. To others, the job serves primarily as the vehicle for satisfying their material needs and is not of overriding importance. Similarly, people differ significantly in their abilities, intelligence, and personality characteristics. As a result, some can take on a greater role in their companies and assume additional responsibilities, while others must have fairly close and supportive direction from management.

Reality-Centered Management recognizes these individual differences. Accordingly, it does not advocate any single leadership style as being appropriate for all employees in all instances. Reality-Centered Management instead calls for a flexible and adaptable management approach reflecting conditions as they actually exist.

For Reality-Centered Management to be successfully implemented in an organization, it must be part of a total systems approach that includes the following five components:

1. *Personnel selection and placement.* A successful staffing system is needed to assure that qualified and motivated personnel are hired.

2. *Employee training and development.* Personnel must be

properly trained, so that they will be able to perform at appropriately productive levels. Part of their training should promote positive work attitudes, so that employees will value quality, customer service, and excellence in job performance.

3. *A sound employee performance appraisal program.* An objective, accurate employee performance appraisal program must be developed to provide factual information about employees' current work performance and clearly indicate specific areas where improvement is required.

4. *Effective ongoing supervision and direction.* The heart of Reality-Centered Management is continuous supervision and direction from management that will result in a high level of productivity. As part of such a strategy, management should use a leadership style that is appropriate to the work situation, and that at all times sets high standards for work performance, accompanied by management's insistence that these standards be met.

5. *An equitable reward and compensation system.* In order for Reality-Centered Management to function in the manner intended, a company must have an equitable compensation system that clearly rewards the achievements and contributions of its personnel.

Each of these five components of an effective Reality-Centered Management system will be discussed in the following chapter.

MANAGEMENT STYLE QUESTIONNAIRE
BY ERWIN S. STANTON, PH.D.

Instructions:
Read each statement and indicate your opinion by placing a check mark in the appropriate column. Since viewpoints on management practices vary from one person to another, there obviously are no "right" or "wrong" answers.

Check One

	STRONGLY AGREE	GENERALLY AGREE	GENERALLY DISAGREE	STRONGLY DISAGREE	POINT VALUE
1. I create a climate in which my subordinates tend to be very cautious rather than risk-taking.	( )	( )	( )	( )	_____
2. I feel that within our department we have too many meetings.	( )	( )	( )	( )	_____
3. In most cases, I believe my people should be encouraged to determine themselves how to accomplish their objectives and not rely upon me.	( )	( )	( )	( )	_____
4. When I give an assignment, I'm inclined to spell out quite clearly how the job is to be done.	( )	( )	( )	( )	_____
5. I give my people a lot of freedom in carrying out their work activities.	( )	( )	( )	( )	_____
6. I usually tell my people the goals or objectives that I want them to attain during the coming year.	( )	( )	( )	( )	_____
7. My superiors expect me to make most of the decisions in my department.	( )	( )	( )	( )	_____

	STRONGLY AGREE	GENERALLY AGREE	GENERALLY DISAGREE	STRONGLY DISAGREE	POINT VALUE

8. Management *must* manage; managers must give definite direction to their subordinates. ( ) ( ) ( ) ( ) ——

9. I believe that people should have a say in work decisions and plans that affect them. ( ) ( ) ( ) ( ) ——

10. I think that, as a rule, most people have the ability to take on additional responsibility on the job. ( ) ( ) ( ) ( ) ——

11. To be frank, I am usually less comfortable when I let my people do things in their own way rather than the way I would have done them. ( ) ( ) ( ) ( ) ——

12. I usually run the department as I see fit and pay only slight attention to my people's suggestions. ( ) ( ) ( ) ( ) ——

13. My people frequently approach me with ideas and recommendations. ( ) ( ) ( ) ( ) ——

14. Basically, my people lack the capacity to get more involved in the running of the department. ( ) ( ) ( ) ( ) ——

15. I frequently give in to my people in discussions with them. ( ) ( ) ( ) ( ) ——

16. As a rule, I feel that my own ideas are generally better than those of my people. ( ) ( ) ( ) ( ) ——

	STRONGLY AGREE	GENERALLY AGREE	GENERALLY DISAGREE	STRONGLY DISAGREE	POINT VALUE
17. I respond readily to changes proposed by my people.	( )	( )	( )	( )	___
18. I feel that, as a manager, I am expected to demonstrate strong, firm, and definite leadership in dealing with my people.	( )	( )	( )	( )	___
19. I frequently compromise on work procedures with my people.	( )	( )	( )	( )	___
20. I usually determine precisely what shall be done and how it will be done by the people under me.	( )	( )	( )	( )	___
21. I insist, as a rule, that people under me follow my instructions to the letter.	( )	( )	( )	( )	___
22. I believe in getting the ideas of my people before proceeding in a given direction.	( )	( )	( )	( )	___
23. I usually insist that things be done my way.	( )	( )	( )	( )	___
24. I frequently change work procedures when my people convince me with the evidence.	( )	( )	( )	( )	___
25. I usually conduct myself in a firm, definite and authoritative manner.	( )	( )	( )	( )	___
26. I usually encourage new ideas from my people.	( )	( )	( )	( )	___

	STRONGLY AGREE	GENERALLY AGREE	GENERALLY DISAGREE	STRONGLY DISAGREE	POINT VALUE
27. As a rule, I think my people get their greatest satisfaction from their families, hobbies, and off-the-job activities.	( )	( )	( )	( )	___
28. I encourage people under me to do their work as they see fit.	( )	( )	( )	( )	___
29. My people's ideas regarding the work of our department are almost as good as my own.	( )	( )	( )	( )	___
30. I generally encourage initiative and innovation in my people.	( )	( )	( )	( )	___

Total Score: _____

SCORING INSTRUCTIONS

To score your responses to the items on the questionnaire, look in the table on the next page for the point values for each question and place those values in the "Point Value" column beside each of the questionnaire items. For example, if you checked the "Generally Agree" column for question No. 1, place the value of 2 points in the "Point Value" column. If, on the other hand, you checked "Strongly Disagree," mark the value of 4 points in the column. When you have finished scoring all the items, add their point values to arrive at your total score.

Reality-Centered People Management

Point Values

QUESTION	STRONGLY AGREE	GENERALLY AGREE	GENERALLY DISAGREE	STRONGLY DISAGREE
1	(1)	(2)	(3)	(4)
2	(1)	(2)	(3)	(4)
3	(4)	(3)	(2)	(1)
4	(1)	(2)	(3)	(4)
5	(4)	(3)	(2)	(1)
6	(1)	(2)	(3)	(4)
7	(1)	(2)	(3)	(4)
8	(1)	(2)	(3)	(4)
9	(4)	(3)	(2)	(1)
10	(4)	(3)	(2)	(1)
11	(1)	(2)	(3)	(4)
12	(1)	(2)	(3)	(4)
13	(4)	(3)	(2)	(1)
14	(1)	(2)	(3)	(4)
15	(4)	(3)	(2)	(1)
16	(1)	(2)	(3)	(4)
17	(4)	(3)	(2)	(1)
18	(1)	(2)	(3)	(4)
19	(4)	(3)	(2)	(1)
20	(1)	(2)	(3)	(4)
21	(1)	(2)	(3)	(4)
22	(4)	(3)	(2)	(1)
23	(1)	(2)	(3)	(4)
24	(4)	(3)	(2)	(1)
25	(1)	(2)	(3)	(4)
26	(4)	(3)	(2)	(1)
27	(1)	(2)	(3)	(4)
28	(4)	(3)	(2)	(1)
29	(4)	(3)	(2)	(1)
30	(4)	(3)	(2)	(1)

5
Applying Reality-Centered Management to Improve Productivity

❧

Previous chapters have discussed the problem of declining productivity and the serious threat it poses to the standard of living of every American. Unquestionably, if we are to reverse the current trend and revitalize our nation's traditionally powerful and productive economy, concerted, coordinated, multidimensional action will be necessary. Reality-Centered Management of an organization's human resources can comprise a significant part of the overall solution.

To a great extent, Reality-Centered Management signals a return to some of the basics of business management, which lately have been deemphasized in far too many organizations. I believe that for some time now many managers and executives have become overly enamored with certain glamorous management concepts, ultrahumanistic movements, and idealistic, if somewhat unrealistic, philosophies. In the process, they have often lost their direction and drifted away from sound management practices. Numerous organizations have paid a steep price for this in the form of declining productivity and overall personnel performance. The time has come for many organizations and many managers to reinstate and, where necessary, update some of their traditional management skills and techniques that have recently remained dormant.

In order to put Reality-Centered Management to work in a practical, results-oriented fashion, more attention must be focused on the following five essential functions:

Effective personnel selection and placement.

Appropriate employee training and development.

Sound employee performance appraisal programs.

Effective ongoing supervision and direction.

Equitable employee reward and compensation systems.

We shall explore each of these management activities in this chapter.

Personnel Selection and Placement

Proper selection and placement of employees is so essential to the success of any organization that it is probably impossible to overstate its importance. In recent years, much attention has been given to the training and development of personnel. While this is, of course, a vital management function, it should be recognized that any training and development that is given to unsatisfactory employees—in essence to those who should never have been hired in the first place—will unquestionably fall on fallow soil and be mostly, if not totally, wasted.

It must also be remembered that hiring and particularly training employees has become a very expensive process. It is estimated that it currently costs a company approximately $2,500 to select and train the *average* employee before such a person ever becomes useful to the organization. Averages, of course, do not tell the whole story. Many companies spend a good deal more than $2,500 before they get any real mileage out of an employee. For example, Wall Street brokerage firms now spend close to $25,000 in hiring and, more important, in training candidates to become brokers before they can effect their very first securities transaction. Sometimes the figures go even higher. One of my insurance company clients recently told me that his organization invests $40,000 in hiring and training each sales representative for its rather sophisticated estate-planning program before any tangible return is ever realized.

The more important the job, the greater will be a company's financial stake in a candidate before there is any appreciable return. In fact, recognizing the complex, technological nature of business today and the relatively long turnaround time needed to evaluate the success of a given project, it is by no means unusual for a company to have invested several years of employment in a managerial, professional, or executive candidate before being able to accurately determine whether that individual should have been hired in the first place. For this reason, before selecting managerial or executive applicants, many companies have them evaluated by a consulting industrial psychologist to determine the likelihood of their future success by means of comprehensive in-depth interviews and selected psychological tests. (Typical psychological evaluations of two actual executive applicants may be found in the Appendix.)

Customarily, then, a fairly extended period of initial training must take place before a new employee becomes truly productive and can be effectively used in a company. Put another way, it is rare that a newly hired person automatically becomes an "instant performer." Hence, the importance of good initial personnel selection.

Another reason why personnel selection has taken on

added significance in recent years is the dramatic change that has occurred in the composition of the nation's labor force. Until the mid-1970s, the United States basically had a manufacturing and production-oriented economy, whose productivity was predominantly determined by the application of technology, machinery, and industrial equipment rather than by the input of its employees. Lately, however, this situation has changed considerably. We have become a *service-oriented* society, with the services being performed more by people than by technology.

Indeed, well over half our gross national product and approximately 70 percent of the nation's labor force is currently engaged in rendering services. Note, for example, the sharp increase over the last several years in the number of people employed in such expanding industries as banking, credit, finance, advertising, electronic data processing, health care, and education, with a corresponding decline in such traditional fields as manufacturing and processing. Since services are basically performed by people, it immediately becomes clear how essential it is to select personnel who are competent, properly qualified for their positions, and appropriately motivated to assure a high level of work performance.

A related aspect of the selection problem involves the promotion process. Virtually all companies attempt, wherever possible, to promote people from within the organization as better positions open up. There are numerous advantages to such a policy. Probably the most significant is the positive effect it has on the morale and motivation of many employees. They can see that good performance will be rewarded, and competent people will advance in the company.

However, major problems frequently occur in organizations where inadequate attention has been paid to the selection process. While reasonably qualified personnel may have been hired initially for the positions then available, all too often these individuals lack the intelligence, ability, and other essential qualifications which would permit them to advance to more responsible positions as they become available. In essence, even though such people could handle the specific positions for which they were hired, they simply were not promotable. This makes it necessary for the organization to go outside to select qualified candidates—a move which usually incurs higher personnel recruiting and selection costs and frequently prompts disappointment, resentment, and lowered morale on the part of those employees who had to be passed over for the promotion. It is therefore essential for companies to emphasize good recruiting and selection if they are to have an adequate reserve of qualified personnel from which to draw as higher-level positions open up.

It appears likely that in the future it is going to become even more difficult to recruit and select competent people. The competition for qualified personnel has always been keen, because there are usually more jobs available for truly capable applicants than there are people seeking them. But beyond that, as we have seen from the data presented in Chapter 3, in the coming years, management will in all probability see a further decline in both the number and quality of ambitious, work-motivated, upward-aspiring job applicants at all levels and in all functional disciplines. Since companies must nevertheless staff their organizations, they will be forced to compete vigorously and imaginatively with other companies to obtain personnel from a smaller pool of desirable and productive applicants than has heretofore existed. For this reason, effective personnel recruiting and selection will become even more critical in the future than it has been in the past.*

* For detailed information on how to install an effective personnel recruiting and selection program, interested readers may wish to consult Erwin S. Stanton, *Successful Personnel Recruiting and Selection* (New York: AMACOM, 1977).

Let us now turn our attention to some of the specific considerations which enter into the personnel selection and placement process from a Reality-Centered Management perspective. It is obviously important that each job applicant possess the requisite intelligence, experience, skills, and other critical qualifications needed for a particular position. However, proper selection and placement must also ake into account the actual setting in which the work will be done.

As we have seen in the last chapter, some jobs are performed in relatively or even highly structured, clearly defined, and unambiguous work environments. In such cases, the work is frequently quite standardized and involves carrying out specific and established duties in a prescribed manner. Moreover, the employee ordinarily is not expected to demonstrate very much originality, initiative, or creativity. Significantly, such assignments can best be handled by those job applicants who derive satisfaction from established, routine, and predictable work settings, and who perform best and feel most comfortable when provided with a relatively high degree of directive supervision.

On the other hand, managers will frequently have to fill openings of a completely different nature. Here the work environment may be highly dynamic, quite unstructured, and often rather ambiguous. Unexpected problems are likely to arise regularly where employees cannot readily fall back on company policy or precedent to guide them. A certain amount of initiative, resourcefulness, and adaptability on the part of employees is required. Such assignments clearly call for a different type of job candidate than the previous situation—one who tends to perform better in a more participative management atmosphere.

In short, it is imperative that job applicants be properly qualified with respect to all the essential criteria. If we are to ensure adequate productivity, it is also critical that we determine that candidates are truly motivated to perform and are prepared to make a contribution to the company. But most important, capable managers will be aware of the differences in work settings that exist in the various jobs under their jurisdiction. They will strive to fit the right person into each assignment, recognizing that some employees thrive in a highly structured environment under directive supervision, while others perform more capably when they can demonstrate their own creativity, imagination, and resourcefulness under a more participative management style.

Employee Training and Development

All employees at all levels periodically need training. This holds as true for experienced executives first joining a company or taking on new assignments with their present company, as it does for entry-level high school or college graduates just beginning their careers. As previously mentioned, it is quite rare that any newly hired person becomes an "instant performer." Indeed, in our dynamic, fast-paced, and rapidly changing technological society, it is essential that companies develop and maintain effective training programs, not only to prepare personnel for their present jobs, but also to keep them up-to-date with changing technology so they will be able to successfully handle future assignments.

Attitude Development

Most companies maintain well-designed and properly conducted training and development programs that deal with conceptual and cognitive information and provide employees with the skills and techniques necessary to effectively carry out their jobs. However, as has been pointed out, one of the chief problems facing American business today is not that people lack the basic *knowledge* to perform their work effectively. Rather, we are dealing here with a problem of *attitude* and the resultant urgent need to instill in our employees appropriate work attitudes that will bring about definite and substantial improvements in performance and productivity.

People bring with them to their jobs work attitudes that by and large are already formed as a result of the experiences to which they have been exposed. Probably the key factor influencing employees' overall work attitudes is the home environment and the ethical standards which were stressed during their more formative years. Similarly, but in all likelihood to a lesser extent, employees' formal training in high school and college may have had some impact.

Actually, some people say that, by the time employees are hired, it is probably already too late: Their values are pretty well formed, and it may be fruitless for a company to attempt to foster the right work attitudes then. Nevertheless, I feel that attitude development is an essential management task. This is a message we must get across if we are to properly use human resources to achieve organizational goals.

Attitude development is really a two-way street. It presupposes obligations on the part of both employees and management. Management, for its part, certainly has a responsibility to treat employees with respect, consideration, and dignity and to offer a comprehensive employee relations program that, among other factors, includes fair compensation, customary employee benefits, and safe working conditions. At the same time, however, as already stated, I believe employees also have an obligation to their organizations. This includes working conscientiously, giving a high-quality job performance, demonstrating having the employer's interests at heart, and making a commitment to attain company goals and objectives.

Granted that this array of employee obligations may sound somewhat old-fashioned and a bit utopian. I think it nevertheless remains a fundamental business truth, relevant to current realities. Moreover, if we are to truly revitalize our economic system, such a return to basics which requires all employees to really put their shoulders to the wheel is, in my opinion, unquestionably called for. The I-don't-give-a-damn attitude is simply unacceptable if productivity is to be restored.

How can management get this message across to its people? I realize it is easier said than done: There is no simple way to instill this attitude. However, management, through its communications and actions, and more specifically, managers, through their daily interactions with their people, must get employees to realize the interests they share with the company. Employees must recognize that the company cannot continue to provide employment unless it functions at a high level of productivity; and that both employees and the organization have specific mutual obligations and responsibilities.

What About the "New Breed" of Employees?

For the past several years, numerous social scientists and their journalist colleagues have been telling us a good deal—often in glowing terms—about the "new breed" of employees. This group, which was born in the 1950s and 1960s during a time of notable social change and grew to maturity in the 1970s, will, we are told, profoundly influence both current and future business thinking and likely cause major changes in the manner in which work will be performed and the way organizations will be structured.

Various articles have appeared in the popular press describing the characteristics of this new breed, some of which I believe have contributed to the decline in productivity and work performance troubling our country. These employees, who generally grew up during a period of relative affluence, are, we are told, very hedonistic, concerned mostly with their own comforts and welfare. Their interests focus predominantly on self and personal satisfactions, with comparatively little attention given to any other considerations.

It is also said that the new breed of employees place great emphasis on instant gratification: They want it all now. Significantly, work for them plays a far less important role in the totality of their lives than leisure-time activities. Furthermore, the new breed of employees are characterized as being strongly influenced by the prevailing psychology of entitlement. They believe they have a right to be given more and more by their employers but at the same time do not necessarily feel they owe any reciprocal obligation to their companies. As a result, we typically have a situation where the new breed of employees want more from their companies in return for less.

In this connection, it seems that management is also being told that the traditional work ethic and its related values are outdated, if not actually dead—that the established work concepts are old-fashioned and irrelevant to today's world. The message is that business is generally out of step, that the values of the new breed of employees are basically correct, and that today's new breed is the forerunner of tomorrow's work force. Accordingly, we cannot expect such employees to adapt to yesterday's work ethic. Instead, if companies are to remain viable, they will need to drastically adapt to accommodate the new type of employees.

The key questions, however, are: How accurate is this assessment of the employees of tomorrow? How sound is the advice being given to business? In my opinion, not very. But more important, I think some of the recommendations being offered are very likely to lead companies in an entirely wrong direction. They are apt to precipitate further deterioration in work productivity and consequently will in no way resolve the problem.

As we have already seen in Chapter 3, employees tend to

vary considerably. In all probability, *the* new breed of employees does not even exist. Rather, management is currently seeing, and undoubtedly will continue to see, a high degree of variability among their employees: Qualifications and work motivation will differ. Indeed as the Yankelovich data indicate, a large number of people are, regrettably, turned off by work. They lack basic job motivation and are essentially leisure oriented. At the same time, however, we must not lose sight of the fact that, fortunately, many employees still *do* respond to traditional work values and ethics. They are dedicated and committed to their companies and have the desire and, more significantly, the capability to make worthwhile contributions to their organizations.

As stated earlier in this chapter, the extent of employee variability underscores the critical importance of proper initial personnel selection. Those job applicants who display inadequate work motivation simply must be screened out. In addition, vigorous recruitment programs should be maintained to ensure that a large number of potentially desirable and contributing job applicants who do subscribe to traditional work values are continually attracted to the company.

Beyond that, sound management requires establishing appropriate standards of job performance and seeing to it that these standards are consistently met. It would be exceedingly regrettable for management to accept lower employee work standards and tolerate less than a truly productive level of performance. Indeed, it is essential for management to make clear to its employees that both they and the company have many mutual interests—that the only way the company can profitably stay in business and guarantee its people steady and satisfactory employment is by maintaining a high rate of productivity. It is therefore vital that employees realize they have definite responsibilities and obligations to the company, in the same way that the company has reciprocal responsibilities and obligations to its employees.

There are a variety of techniques and methods management can use on a continuous basis to ensure that performance goals and objectives are attained. Strategies that can help managers meet established targets include the proper use of performance appraisals, effective ongoing supervision and direction, and an equitable reward and compensation program. We shall deal more fully with each of these techniques in the balance of this chapter.

Employee Performance Appraisal

One of the most effective tools available to managers in implementing Reality-Centered Management is the employee performance appraisal. This technique is not new: Most companies have long had a variety of programs that evaluate and appraise the performance of employees with varying degrees of success. At the same time, such programs have not always been popular with managers. All too often, they fail to see the value of the technique and instead regard the evaluation procedure as cumbersome, too time-consuming, and frequently not particularly productive.

Nevertheless, performance appraisal programs have the potential to be exceedingly useful management tools, both to serve administrative purposes as well as to assist in the training and development of employees. The major advantages of a sound, professionally administered employee performance appraisal program are that it can:

1. Identify specific areas where companywide training is needed.
2. Further the individual training and development of employees.

3. Assist in gathering vital information for a human resources inventory system.
4. Provide an objective basis for compensation.
5. Facilitate more objective decision making about employee promotions, demotions, transfers, and discharges.
6. Improve employee morale and motivation by permitting individuals to know precisely where they stand.
7. Help build a better relationship between managers and employees.
8. Facilitate compliance with government equal employment opportunity requirements by focusing on essential, legally defensible, and job-related performance criteria.

For the performance appraisal program to assist in the training and development of employees, it is vital that managers fully involve employees in the total process. One of the major reasons why performance appraisals have not always been successful in business and industry is that all too often they are too one-sided. Managers play the only active role, while employees remain relatively passive and fail to get adequately involved in the process. As a result, the appraisees do not become truly committed to improving their work performance.

The primary purpose of the appraisal process is to improve the job performance of employees—in essence, to effect changes in their behavior. One of the cardinal psychological principles regarding learning and behavior change is that people tend to attain those goals that they themselves have helped formulate and to which they have consequently become committed. We shall shortly review a performance appraisal strategy in which both managers and appraisees play active roles, and which, as a result, is more likely to bring about definite performance improvement in employees.

The performance appraisal program is actually a two-stage process. The first calls for gathering relevant and objective information about the employees' most recent job performance, and it is here that managers play the key role. As vital information is collected, it provides a factual basis to assist management in making certain personnel decisions (involving, for example, salary increases, promotions, and transfers to other assignments), as previously noted.

It is, however, in the second stage, particularly in the course of conducting the performance appraisal interview, that the training and development process is enhanced. Here the manager and employee jointly review the appraisee's most recent performance—customarily for a period covering the past six months to a year—to determine what improvements are needed. Both then agree on and commit themselves to certain concrete steps that will achieve the desired goals and objectives. The two stages of an effective performance appraisal program will now be examined at greater length.

Obtaining Performance Appraisal Data

In gathering information regarding the appraisee's most recent performance, it is vital that managers focus their evaluation exclusively on essential and objective employee behavior that is directly linked to success in the position. Indeed, since so many personnel decisions are ultimately influenced by if not actually based on performance appraisals, it is essential that managers abide by this cardinal rule if they are to comply with current federal equal employment opportunity requirements.

Such personal traits as a friendly manner or a good sense of humor are almost invariably irrelevant to job success and accordingly would not constitute legally defensible criteria for performance evaluation under government guidelines. At the same time, however, an appraisal comment describing an accountant as being typically late in furnishing needed data for the monthly financial statement would be highly pertinent and certainly directly related to job success.

In gathering objective input for employee performance appraisals, managers often have various sources of information to assist them. To begin with, employees' job descriptions frequently offer a good initial reference point. In addition, many organizations have developed concrete standards which spell out precisely what constitutes successful job performance. Various factual data are also frequently available to aid managers, such as employee production records, sales representatives' sales figures, or figures on the number of new accounts opened since the last appraisal period.

Finally, in collecting information, many managers have found it invaluable to use a technique known as the "critical incident method." Here managers not only identify the relevant facts but also provide specific examples of employees' recent job performance that were typical of their customary behavior and representative of essential or critical actions which the employees performed or failed to perform.

Critical incidents can include successful as well as unsuccessful employee behavior. An example of a positive critical incident for a sales representative would be that her monthly expense reports were customarily both accurate and submitted on time. A negative critical incident for a statistical typist, on the other hand, might be that her work frequently needed to be redone because of major errors. One of the chief advantages of including critical incidents in the performance appraisal is that they provide very concrete and specific illustrations of actual past events to which managers can refer as part of the evaluation interview in order to help employees improve their future work.

In order to improve the rating process, literally thousands of performance appraisal forms have been designed following a variety of formats and conceptual models. Some of these forms have been quite elaborate, cumbersome, and time-consuming to complete, without, however, having accomplished their purpose. This probably accounts for the unpopularity of the appraisal process with many managers. Nevertheless, we should not lose sight of the potential value of a well-designed and properly functioning employee performance appraisal program: It need not be a cumbersome or futile exercise in paperwork for managers. In fact, I strongly recommend a fairly simple and straightforward approach that essentially calls for actual job performance descriptions and evaluative comments by both managers and employees regarding the employees' recent job behavior. We shall see how such a program can be effectively implemented in the next section.

Using Performance Appraisals as a Training and Development Tool

Let us now focus on how a properly designed performance appraisal program can help in training and developing employees. To prepare the necessary input information as well as lay the groundwork for the subsequent appraisal interview, the manager should complete the Employee Performance Review, of which Figure 1 is a prototype. At the same time, in order to begin the process by which the employee also becomes actively involved in the appraisal program, he or she likewise is asked to complete a rating form, in this case, the Employee Career Review, of which Figure 2 is a prototype.

Readers will note that the two review forms are identical, with the exception of the last item. The manager's form reads "Anticipated Future Potential," enabling the reviewer to indicate an overall assessment of the employee's projected future. The appraisee's form reads "Future Career Goals," enabling the employee to indicate the di-

FIGURE 1.

EMPLOYEE PERFORMANCE REVIEW

Name of Employee _____ Date _____

Department _____ Position _____

Date of Employment _____ Time in Present Position _____

Comprehensive Description of Job Performance During the Past Year:

Key Accomplishments During the Past Year:

Significant Difficulties and/or Problems Encountered:

Recommended Job-Related Goals for the Coming Year:

Recommended Personal Development Goals for the Coming Year:

Areas of Greatest Strength:

Areas Requiring Additional Development:

Anticipated Future Potential:

Signatures:

Individual Rated _____ Date _____

Reviewer _____ Date _____

Reviewer's Superior _____ Date _____

FIGURE 2.
EMPLOYEE CAREER REVIEW

Name of Employee _____ Date _____

Department _____ Position _____

Date of Employment _____ Time in Present Position _____

Comprehensive Description of Job Performance During the Past Year:

Key Accomplishments During the Past Year:

Significant Difficulties and/or Problems Encountered:

Recommended Job-Related Goals for the Coming Year:

Recommended Personal Development Goals for the Coming Year:

Areas of Greatest Strength:

Areas Requiring Additional Development:

Future Career Goals:

Signatures:

Employee _____ Date _____

Superior _____ Date _____

rection of his or her career interests. The paperwork should be distributed several days prior to the scheduled performance appraisal interview to allow adequate preparation time for both the manager and the employee.

It should again be stressed that the information the manager generates on the Employee Performance Review Form must be objective and totally job related. In addition, the manager's evaluation of the employee should, in turn, be reviewed and approved by his or her superior. In fact, in some organizations, in order to make certain that an employee has been objectively appraised, a committee of three persons is used to evaluate each individual's performance.

Conducting the Appraisal Interview

From a training and development perspective, the most important aspect of the performance appraisal process is the feedback interview between the manager and the employee. It is here that the appraisees can be helped to improve their work and, hopefully, be encouraged to commit themselves to a concrete course of action that will result in performance improvement. Yet more often than not, the feedback interview goes very badly, and both the manager and the employee are disappointed in the results. Because of the failure of past evaluation interviews, managers are often extremely reluctant to conduct such sessions. In many instances, managers will avoid them if possible, thus losing a prime opportunity to enhance the performance of their people.

However, most management specialists firmly believe that the evaluation interview is an essential part of a manager's job. With proper training, managers unquestionably can gain the skills necessary to conduct good evaluation interviews that will help their subordinates improve their work performance. Let us see, then, how the evaluation interview can be successfully conducted.

To begin with, both the manager and the employee need to properly prepare for this important meeting. Consequently, it is suggested that the interview be scheduled in advance, and that both parties know what they want to accomplish in the forthcoming discussion. Because it is likely that the employee will feel a certain tension and anxiety, it is important that the manager possess the necessary interviewing skills to establish rapport with the appraisee and put him or her at complete ease. What should follow is a thorough discussion of the employee's recent job performance, with both the manager and the appraisee referring to the Employee Performance Review and the Employee Career Review forms (Figures 1 and 2), which were completed in preparation for the meeting.

The entire focus of the appraisal interview should be on the future: It should not dwell excessively on the past. More significantly, the interview should stress what specific steps the employee will wish to take to upgrade his or her performance. Where there have been problems and difficulties in the past, these should serve primarily as reference points illustrating what has been learned from them to make certain that they will not be repeated, as well as how in the future the employee can profit from these mistakes or incorrect approaches. Critical incidents, to which we have previously referred, can be used to best advantage here by providing the employee with explicit and concrete examples to help him or her improve future work performance.

If the evaluation interview is to succeed as a training and development tool, it is vital that both parties see eye to eye on essential performance standards, on exactly what is expected of the employee, and most critically, on precisely what steps the appraisee needs to take in order to meet established standards. Any discussion of personality traits or characteristics not directly related to the job should be strenuously avoided. Likewise, the manager should never compare the appraisee with other employees. He or she should instead stress the essential performance standards needed for success in the job, and what the employee must do to meet them.

The most successful evaluation interviews result when *both* the manager and the employee play a very active role in the meeting, and there is a frank discussion of past problems and difficulties and required corrective action. Once again, it is here that the manager's interviewing skills will serve most ably, particularly if he or she can successfully draw out the employee in conversation and fully understand the employee's point of view.

The manager must be forthright and honest with the employee, with the emphasis during the entire meeting being on openness and candor and good two-way communication taking place between the parties. The manager also should make every effort to listen carefully to what the employee has to say. Frequently the appraisee will express the need for additional support or assistance from the manager, who should be prepared to give assurances that such help will be forthcoming, if it appears appropriate.

As we have seen repeatedly in this book, employees vary in their ability to participate with management in most activities. This applies equally to evaluation interviews. Some people by nature will take a very active part in such discussions; others will tend to be more passive, expecting the manager to play the directive role. Once again, the manager will need to be flexible enough to effectively deal with both types of employee and adapt to the varying situations which are likely to arise.

Of critical importance, however—and this cannot be overemphasized—is that employees clearly understand what is expected of them on the job, that they know what specific steps are needed to improve work performance, and that they be committed to taking these essential steps. The manager, by using his or her coaching skills, must successfully encourage the employee to make such a commitment. To assist the appraisee in this connection, the manager can frequently point out the tangible rewards that may result from improved performance (for example, anticipated salary increases or consideration for possible future promotion).

When the employee has not made a sincere commitment to meeting performance standards and agreed-upon goals, however, it is most unlikely that he or she will ever be sufficiently motivated to attain them. Many authorities believe that the very essence of good management is the manager's ability to get the employee to make this commitment. The appraisal meeting should end on a positive and optimistic note, with the employee feeling confident that he or she will be able to achieve the goals to which both the employee and the manager have committed themselves.

To check yourself on how successful you were in conducting the performance appraisal interview, you might reflect on the following points:

1. Specifically what was accomplished?
2. Were the *real* problems brought out? What were they?
3. Was there a good manager–employee relationship?
   a. Was there openness and leveling?
   b. Was there mutual respect?
   c. How well did the two parties communicate?
   d. Was the superior perceived as a helper, or as a punitive judge?
4. Was there mutual job understanding?
5. Was there a joint setting of *performance objectives*?
6. Was there a definite joint *commitment* for performance improvement?
7. How did each person feel about the meeting?

If you are not satisfied with the results of your performance appraisal interviews, you might wish to focus on developing your skill in this vital management area.

Ongoing Supervision and Direction

The success of Reality-Centered Management of a company's human resources as a means of increasing organizational productivity and assisting in revitalization depends predominantly on effective and continuous managerial supervision. This is the heart of Reality-Centered Management. In many ways, such effective, ongoing direction is an outgrowth of the principles and concepts underlying a successfully managed performance appraisal system. It requires a managerial strategy which I call Managing for Productivity Results.

The Managing for Productivity Results System is illustrated in Figure 3. The system begins at Point 1 on the cycle, with the manager and the employee both fully understanding and agreeing upon the essential requirements of the employee's job, and committing themselves to achieving the goals and objectives necessary for a high level of performance. In order for the objectives to be met, they should be stated in specific terms and be both realistic and reasonably attainable. It is essential that the objectives be set at an appropriate level, for if they are set too high, employees are apt to become dismayed and disillusioned at their inability to meet the targets, and if they are set too low, both the company and the employees are shortchanged. The company will fail to get sufficient productivity, and employees will fail to gain any real job satisfaction if their abilities are not adequately challenged.

The cycle now turns to Point 2, with the employee making progress toward attaining the mutually agreed-upon goals and objectives. Such progress is apt to be more read-

FIGURE 3.

MANAGING FOR PRODUCTIVITY RESULTS SYSTEM

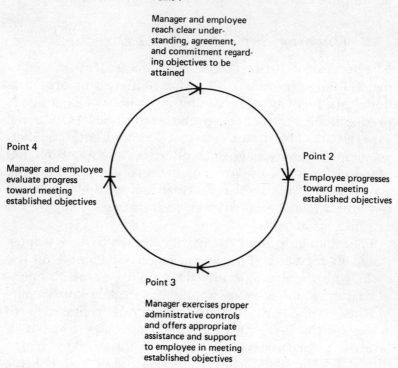

Point 1

Manager and employee
reach clear under-
standing, agreement,
and commitment regard-
ing objectives to be
attained

Point 4

Manager and employee
evaluate progress
toward meeting
established objectives

Point 2

Employee progresses
toward meeting
established objectives

Point 3

Manager exercises proper
administrative controls
and offers appropriate
assistance and support
to employee in meeting
established objectives

ily forthcoming because the employee has played an active role in the process. Consequently, the employee is motivated largely because he or she has made a commitment to achieving the goal and therefore has a personal stake in the results.

As the cycle continues through Point 3, the manager continually exercises appropriate administrative controls and provides whatever support and assistance are necessary to help the employee achieve established objectives. Finally, at Point 4, the manager and the employee evaluate the progress that has been made by comparing the actual results against the specific objectives originally set at Point 1. If all, or substantially all, the objectives have been met, and the position requirements remain basically the same, the cycle returns to Point 1, with a restatement and reaffirmation of previously agreed-upon goals and objectives. If the goals and objectives have not been satisfactorily met, however, or if the requirements of the position have changed, then at Point 1 the manager and the employee must once again reach a clear understanding, agreement, and commitment regarding the new objectives. And so the cycle continues in the manner just indicated.

In order for a Managing for Productivity Results System to work effectively, the following essential requirements must be met:

1. There must be a thorough understanding of job requirements.
2. There must be a clear understanding of performance objectives.
3. There must be continuous interaction between the manager and the employee.
4. There must be a good manager-employee relationship.
5. There must be effective supervision and enforcement of discipline.

These requirements will now be discussed briefly.

Job Understanding

Both the manager and the employee must have a clear understanding and agreement on basic job requirements. There must also be clarity and agreement on performance standards, particularly as they apply to such essential factors as the quality and quantity of work performed, time requirements for accomplishing the work, and any other critical aspects that comprise effective job performance. And since jobs continually change in a fast-paced technological society, it is essential that performance standards be kept up to date to reflect any recent significant modifications in the position.

Understanding of Performance Objectives

Managers and employees must likewise agree on the specific goals and objectives which employees are expected to meet. Indeed, as we have seen in Chapter 2, one of the basic needs of every individual is for security. This need can be satisfied if employees have a complete knowledge of precisely what is expected of them by their superiors. Moreover, from the point of view of goal attainment, only if employees fully understand the performance standards they are expected to meet are they likely to attain them. It should be stressed once again that performance standards must be set at an appropriately high level, and employees held clearly accountable for their attainment, if satisfactory productivity and organizational revitalization are to be achieved.

Interaction Between Managers and Employees

It is absolutely essential for managers and employees to maintain continuous interaction with each other. Managers, of necessity, must always be informed about current operations in their departments. If unanticipated problems arise, managers will need to take corrective action, often at once. Employees will frequently require specific assistance and support which only the managers can provide. Hence, managers should always be available and, through their attitude, approachable by employees.

Employees will remain distant and aloof from managers who are viewed as punitive judges and will refrain from freely communicating with them. They will often attempt to hide bad news from such managers rather than risk displeasing them and possibly damaging their standing and future in the company. Instead, the managers' role should always be that of helpful coaches to whom people can readily come for assistance in handling job difficulties as they arise. In essence, their posture should be: "What is your problem in meeting targets, and how can I help you?"

Manager–Employee Relationship

To a great extent, what makes the productivity results cycle (Figure 3) move is the lubricant supplied by a good manager-employee relationship. If mutual trust and respect are present, if there is openness and leveling between the two parties, and if good communication exists, then a sound manager-employee relationship should result. As noted, this type of relationship can be facilitated if the manager is viewed by employees as a helper and coach, and if the manager's leadership style is supportive, non-threatening, and problem oriented.

Supervision and Enforcement of Discipline

Ideally, it would be delightful if all employees had the proper attitude, willingness to work, and commitment to organizational goals to perform appropriately and earn their keep. However, we are not living in an ideal world. In the real world of work there will always be some undisciplined, incompetent people who will represent a drain on the company. This will happen, despite our best efforts to properly select employees and despite the best of training programs.

Positive, self-imposed discipline is always preferred in employees. Nevertheless, from time to time, all managers will have people working for them who simply cannot be trained and developed, who cannot or will not perform appropriately and contribute to the organization, or who display negative behavior. It is therefore essential for managers to maintain proper discipline and to set and demand high performance standards. This is especially important if productivity and revitalization efforts are to succeed.

Clearly, every reasonable attempt should be made to straighten out and to train and develop such unsatisfactory employees. Moreover, they should be given adequate warning, be properly informed about management's dissatisfaction, and told what they are expected to do to meet appropriate performance standards. In this context, managers will periodically need to conduct disciplinary interviews. However, eventually the point will be reached with some employees when managers must realize that the situation is hopeless, and that the unsatisfactory employees will need to be discharged.

In the course of my management consulting, I have frequently been amazed at the excessive tolerance shown by some companies, and how often unsatisfactory employees take utter advantage of overly humanistic and well-meaning employers, much to the companies' detriment. I believe very strongly that all managers owe an obligation to the company, its stockholders, customers, and employees to discharge personnel who do not meet appropriate standards of performance and behavior.*

It is somewhat outside the scope of this book to go into a great deal of detail in how to handle disciplinary interviews. Nevertheless, the following suggestions are offered which I have found useful in training managers in how to effectively conduct such sessions with unsatisfactory employees:

---

* In this regard, it is absolutely imperative for managers to maintain adequate records specifying the areas of unsatisfactory employee work performance. Indeed, in view of current equal employment opportunity guidelines and resulting litigation, such detailed documentation has become mandatory.

1. Prepare for the interview:
   a. Thoroughly analyze the problem.
   b. Have all your facts ready.
   c. Know what you want to accomplish.
   d. Arrange for complete privacy.
2. State your case clearly, succinctly, and immediately.
3. Give the employee ample time and opportunity to tell his (her) side of the story.
4. Do not interrupt him (her); do not lose your temper; do not argue with him (her).
5. Stick to the facts; focus on job-related behavior which fails to meet essential performance standards.
6. Have available *critical incidents* of actual job behavior to help illustrate your point.
7. Indicate clearly the seriousness of the problem and state what your expectations are for the future.
8. Try to get a personal commitment for change on the part of the employee.
9. Attempt to have him (her) feel positive about the organization, the department and, hopefully, about you.
10. End the interview on a positive note, indicating your confidence in the employee and his (her) ability to meet performance standards.
11. Maintain a close follow-up to determine if corrective steps are, in fact, being taken and that improvement in work performance is taking place.
12. If no improvement is forthcoming, take prompt steps to discharge the employee.
13. Maintain proper documentation of the entire case.

Reward and Compensation System

If Reality-Centered Management is to increase productivity and further the revitalization of an organization, a sound and equitable reward and compensation system must exist. While this chapter does not aim to offer details on establishing a comprehensive employee compensation program, we should not lose sight of the fact that people must continually be motivated and rewarded for effective work if productive job performance is to be sustained.

A workable and motivating reward and compensation system has a number of essential components. To begin with, salaries in the company must be competitive with those being paid by other comparable organizations in the community. In addition, a sound job evaluation system should be in effect so that more demanding and responsible positions pay higher salaries than assignments of lesser scope, complexity, and magnitude. Furthermore, salary increases should be awarded periodically and should clearly reflect the individual's recent performance and contribution to the company's objectives rather than being increments given out on a purely automatic basis. Succinctly put, those employees who deserve salary increases should get them; those who don't should not.

Other components of a successful and comprehensive reward and compensation system should include, wherever possible, internal promotion, employee profit sharing, and appropriate supplementary benefits that effectively reward employees for good performance. (A case in point is where employees' jobs have been significantly expanded as a result of job-enrichment programs so that they have become more productive. Compensation should be adjusted accordingly to clearly reflect such productivity increases.)

Summary

Organizations can most effectively implement Reality-Centered Management through a program which stresses the essential functions of effective personnel selection and placement, appropriate employee training and development, sound performance appraisal, effective ongoing supervision and direction, and equitable employee reward and compensation. These four components have traditionally formed the foundation of a sound management system to help companies meet their desired goals and objectives. They are key, critical management functions which today are even more essential if we are to succeed in revitalizing our organizations, once again improve our productivity levels, and regain our competitive edge.

6
Reality-Centered Management Looks Ahead

❦

Planning for the Growth and Continuity of the Company

Until now, we have directed our attention exclusively to how Reality-Centered Management can best respond to the immediately pressing problem of improving organizational productivity and individual performance. In so doing, we have emphasized the specific strategies needed to manage our companies' current human resources most effectively. Vital as this may be, Reality-Centered Management cannot limit itself to dealing only with today's urgent problem. Management must look further down the road and plan for the organization's future. This will be the focus of the present chapter.

Successful organizations have long engaged in strategic planning. Such long-range planning has customarily focused in great detail on various functional areas, such as marketing, production, and finance. Surprisingly, however, long-range human resources planning has often been ignored or relatively de-emphasized. The assumption has been that when the company's plans are firmly in place and certain personnel are needed, they will simply be available in the organization; if not, then the company will just have to go out and get them.

As we have seen in the last chapter, however, it is a myth that new employees become "instant performers" the moment they are hired. Instead, truly competent personnel must first be identified and then developed—a process which usually takes time and calls for careful advance planning and preparation. Hence, if a company is to move ahead and take appropriate advantage of its available opportunities, it must make certain that it will have sufficient qualified people on board to properly implement its plans. Indeed, the strategic planning of human resources to ensure their timely availability to the company is as vital as any other aspect of long-range corporate planning and must not be neglected.

The Importance of Organization Planning

Before any *human resources planning* can be done, however, a good deal of *organization planning* must take place. To engage in human resources planning without coordinating the entire process very closely with organization planning would actually be to operate in a vacuum. It would be largely, if not totally, a waste of time. Indeed, until we know very clearly in which direction a company is headed, it is completely impossible to focus realistically on the number and types of people the organization will require. Perhaps Lewis Carroll best expressed this idea in the sage advice he gave in *Alice in Wonderland:* "If you don't know where you are going, any road will take you there."

Some critics have charged that because of the rapidity of events taking place in business—such as unanticipated mergers or acquisitions—it is really not feasible to do any long-range organization planning. I recognize there may be some validity to this charge. However, while unexpected contingencies can frequently arise which will drastically change the scope and nature of a company's long-range strategies, failure to have a definite plan of action invites organizational malaise and will inevitably result in lost business opportunities.

How, then, do we engage in sound organization planning? What specific factors must be taken into account in projecting the company's future? To begin with, the following key questions must be asked:

1. What is the broader business area in which we are currently engaged?
2. What are the new areas of business activity in which we plan to become involved?
3. In which direction do we plan to head? When?
4. What are our plans for growth and expansion?
5. Into which market and territorial areas do we want to expand?
6. What are our plans for expansion in the international area?
7. What changes in organizational structure are likely to result from possible corporate acquisitions, mergers, or consolidations?
8. What major technological changes and developments are likely to occur in the businesses in which we are engaged or anticipate becoming engaged?

Once we have answered some of these critical questions, we should have a good picture of what the company will look like in the future. We should then be ready to ask ourselves whether we have available in the company fully qualified personnel to staff the various positions that will need to be filled in keeping with the direction in which the organization is headed. This is the essence of human resources planning, which will be discussed in the balance of this chapter.

Human Resources Planning

As with the process of organization planning, in focusing on the process of human resources planning, it is helpful to begin by asking some pointed questions. These are:

1. What kinds of professionals, managers, and executives will we need?
2. What specific qualifications will we require?
3. What new skills and qualifications not presently found in the company will we need?
4. What is the overall level of competence of our present professional, managerial, and executive staff?
5. To what extent do we presently have sufficiently qualified personnel in keeping with the anticipated growth and expansion of the company?
6. What personnel losses must be anticipated as a result of resignations, retirements, discharges, or other causes?

Having asked some of these key questions, we should now possess a rather critical and objective assessment of the present quality and future potential of the company's human resources. If throughout the years we have been generally successful in hiring qualified personnel who, in addition to being competent in their present jobs, show a good deal of promise for growth and advancement in the company, then, presumably, we will have an adequate personnel reservoir to staff many higher-level positions as they open up. More typically, however, companies find that while some future openings can undoubtedly be filled from within, in other instances qualified personnel will not be available and outside candidates will need to be secured.

Internal Promotion or External Hiring?

Whenever a new position opens up, or we look ahead to do any serious human resources planning, one question immediately emerges: Shall we fill this opening from within the company, or will we need to bring in a qualified candidate from outside? Looking at this question from a broader perspective, is it better as a general policy to fill openings through internal promotion or through external hiring?

It is extremely difficult to give a definitive answer. The best that can be said is that it all depends upon some rather strategic factors. As a broad generalization, it is usually acknowledged that—all factors being equal—it is better to promote people from within the company than to hire from outside. However, as a rule, all factors are very rarely equal. Let us examine some of the major advantages of each approach.

The biggest benefit of internal promotion is the undisputed positive effect such a practice has on the morale and motivation of people working in the company. It enables employees to see clear-cut evidence that they have a future in the organization, and that good performance will be rewarded through career advancement. In a related vein, if there is tangible evidence that people can move up in the company, they are less apt to explore job opportunities elsewhere. Consequently, employee turnover is likely to be substantially reduced, resulting in significantly lower personnel selection and training costs. Finally, the promoted employee, by virtue of having already worked in the company for a period of time, is relatively familiar with the organization and its policies and procedures and ordinarily will require less orientation and training for the new assignment than a person brought in from the outside.

On the other hand, there are some very persuasive arguments in favor of bringing in fully qualified and experienced people from the outside. This is especially true if it is felt that really competent personnel are not readily available within the organization. Because of a company's recent growth and expansion, for example, its current personnel resources may already have been stretched to the limit; its professional, managerial, and executive staff may be rather sparse.

Another benefit of external hiring is that it enables a company to take immediate advantage of the specialized expertise of highly qualified people who would bring with them some valuable experience obtained in another organization. For example, a company may be planning to expand into a new business area. If a thoroughly experienced individual with a proven track record of accomplishments in such a specialty is hired, the new person could be expected to spearhead the company's projected expansion. Frequently, however, if management is completely candid, it will recognize that the qualifications of some members of the organization simply leave a lot to be desired. Quite bluntly, a company may be dissatisfied with the competence of some of its people. It may conclude that a much higher caliber of personnel must be secured.

Even if a company is relatively pleased with the ability of its personnel, it is usually highly desirable to periodically recruit a certain number of new people from the outside. This is because such individuals often bring some new, different, and perhaps innovative ideas and practices with which they have been working in their former organizations. Because of the high costs associated with doing business as well as the substantial investment that companies make in equipment, processes, and programs, most organizations tend to become rather conservative and often favor the status quo. By introducing new people who may think differently and favor different approaches—"new blood," if you will—a company can frequently reassess its traditional ways of doing things and consider whether they are still relevant, or whether they should be updated and changed.

To return to the strategic question of whether a company should emphasize internal promotion or external hiring, the basic factor that must be taken into account is the organization's assessment of the overall quality of its human resources. If the company is substantially satisfied with the caliber of its current personnel and generally feels that they are qualified to assume more responsible, higher-level positions, then the bulk of future job assignments should be made through internal promotions. On the other hand, if the company is less confident of the ability of its present staff, then it should favor external hiring. As noted, however, a certain mix of internal promotions and external staffing is always highly desirable to avoid a natural tendency toward the inbreeding of existing ideas, approaches, and strategies.

Finally, the following incident, which happened a number of years ago, aptly illustrates the damage that can result from overreliance on internal promotion. At that time, I visited a well-known *Fortune* 500 company in the hope of interesting them in using our firm's executive recruiting service. This particular organization had at one time been the leader in its industry. More recently, it had lost a significant part of its traditional market share and acquired the reputation of being lackluster, unimaginative, and noninnovative. I felt that with a healthy infusion of some qualified people from the outside bringing new ideas, strategies, and approaches, the company could, once again, regain a good portion of its former prominence. When I suggested the advantages of recruiting new talent from the outside, management vigorously protested such a move, exclaiming "But we only promote from within!" The postscript to this story is that, in more recent years, the decline of this once powerful corporate giant has become even more pronounced, with the organization teetering repeatedly on the brink of bankruptcy. One can only speculate how the timely infusion of some qualified new blood might have benefited this company.

Developing a Human Resources Inventory

Companies customarily maintain an accurate inventory of all their important physical assets. Similarly, well-managed organizations should also maintain an up-to-date inventory of what is generally regarded as a company's most valuable if somewhat less tangible asset: its people. As we have already seen in this chapter, if a company develops and maintains an accurate current inventory of its human resources, it will be in a better position to correctly determine whether any specific new job assignment can properly be filled internally or externally. Moreover, a factual, up-to-date human resources inventory will be of immeasurable value in undertaking human resources planning to ensure that qualified personnel will always be available in keeping with the company's plans for future growth and expansion.

I recommend a comprehensive, highly objective, and accurate method for gathering vital information for a human resources inventory—a method that has been successfully implemented by our consulting firm in numerous organizations of various sizes over many years. The chief purpose of the human resources inventory is to provide critical information for management decision making in support of the company's strategic planning programs. Succinctly stated, the human resources inventory ensures that the company will have qualified people precisely when they are needed to implement specific programs.

As indicated in Figure 4, there are two critical components, or data, that comprise a total human resources inventory system. The first is the psychological evaluation conducted by an outside consulting management psychologist; the second is the human resources inventory data supplied by an employee's direct superior. These two components, operating independently but clearly in support of each other, can be expected to provide a wealth of accurate and objective information regarding key personnel to assist management in making important staffing decisions. We will now examine these two components.

The Psychological Evaluation

In the last chapter, we saw how a psychological evaluation by a professional consulting management psychologist can assist a company in initially selecting better personnel. Similarly, a properly conducted psychological evaluation of *currently employed personnel* can also provide management with valuable additional information for a company's total human resources inventory system.

When it comes to using psychological evaluations with *currently employed* individuals, however, a question that occasionally arises is why such a procedure is necessary in the first place. After all, the argument goes, these people are not unknown quantities to the company, as would be the case with job applicants being considered from the outside. These individuals are apt to be experienced managers or professionals who have been with the company for a period of time. As a result, management has already had ample opportunity to assess their performance and potential.

Granted that in well-managed organizations a good deal of vital information is indeed already available regarding personnel. But more often than not, these employees have been functioning in specialized and perhaps somewhat limited settings which may not have given management the opportunity to get a comprehensive view of all their abilities and, more important, their potential. Moreover, as we have seen in the last chapter, performance evaluation data are not always as complete, thorough, or objective as they should be. Hence, the abilities and potential of some highly qualified personnel may never be brought to management's attention.

It is therefore highly advisable for a company to round out its knowledge of key individuals through a supplemental assessment by a totally objective outside management psychologist. Because such psychologists, unlike the assessee's direct superior, have had no previous contact or experience with the candidate which might otherwise introduce a subjective element, they frequently see the person in a completely different light. As a result, they are usually able to provide the company with fresh information and insight about the individual.

In conducting the evaluation, the psychologist traditionally relies upon a rather detailed and comprehensive interview with the individual, supplemented by selected psychological tests which measure specific intellectual, motivational, and personality factors. In the process, the psychologist seeks to fully understand the assessee and all of his or her abilities, interests, and talents. Considerable emphasis is also given to exploring the career and life goals, plans, and aspirations of the individual and how these might be satisfied within the structure of the company.

The psychological evaluation not only assists the organization in its human resources planning but also contributes substantially to the career development of the individual. Indeed, a generally accepted practice is that, shortly after completion of the psychological evaluation, the assessee returns to the psychologist for a review of the findings and a discussion of the steps the individual can take to further his or her own career development.

The psychologist's evaluation findings are normally written up in a detailed report for presentation to management. In the Appendix, readers will find two psychological evaluations which illustrate the type of information such reports can be expected to provide. (In both cases, the significant data on the evaluations have been altered to protect the identities of the individuals involved.) The first sample evaluation is of Martin T. Wilson, a highly promising individual, then employed as a middle-level executive, who was being considered for a significant internal promotion. He was, in fact, subsequently appointed president of a *Fortune* 500 company. Since that time, he has successfully directed this organization's growth, expansion, and impressive profitability. The second sample evaluation is of Peter Sanford, an external applicant who was being considered for an important staff and training assignment an assistant to the president of a leading multinational manufacturing company. Had this candidate been successful, the position would have lead to a divisional general managership in the foreseeable future.

In short, as Figure 4 shows, the consulting management psychologist contributes to the total human resources inventory system by providing comprehensive evaluations of key individuals, identification of their current growth and development needs, and assessments of their future potential with the company.

Human Resources Inventory Data Furnished by the Manager

The second component of the total human resources inventory system consists of data furnished by the individual's immediate superior. Included is the superior's assessment of the employee's current performance, personal growth and development needs, future potential, and possible replacements. This information is designed to establish a dynamic and current picture of the individual as seen by his or her superior.

FIGURE 4.

HUMAN RESOURCES INVENTORY SYSTEM

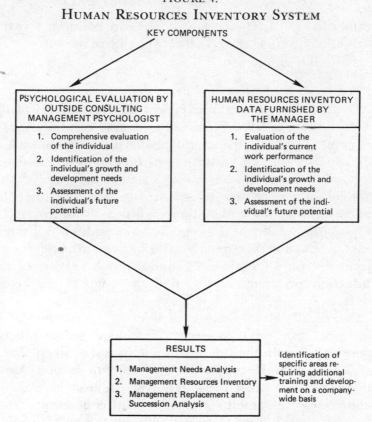

KEY COMPONENTS

PSYCHOLOGICAL EVALUATION BY OUTSIDE CONSULTING MANAGEMENT PSYCHOLOGIST	HUMAN RESOURCES INVENTORY DATA FURNISHED BY THE MANAGER
1. Comprehensive evaluation of the individual 2. Identification of the individual's growth and development needs 3. Assessment of the individual's future potential	1. Evaluation of the individual's current work performance 2. Identification of the individual's growth and development needs 3. Assessment of the individual's future potential

RESULTS

1. Management Needs Analysis
2. Management Resources Inventory
3. Management Replacement and Succession Analysis

Identification of specific areas requiring additional training and development on a company-wide basis

The information periodically generated by the manager as part of the regular performance appraisal program serves as a vital source input in compiling human resources inventory data. The appraisal information is *summarized*, with the focus kept exclusively on providing strategic data regarding the individual's potential for *future advancement* in the company. A sample Human Resources Inventory report follows. It illustrates the type of information that should be provided and the desired emphasis of such a report.

115

Reality-Centered People Management

HUMAN RESOURCES INVENTORY DATA

Name: Joseph T. Hood   Time in Position: 4 years
Title: Plant Manager,   Age: 43 years
    Dallas Operation

Evaluation of Current Performance

Mr. Hood has done an excellent job running his plant, often under rather difficult and adverse conditions. His recommendations for expanding the plant's manufacturing capacity to take advantage of increased demand for our products in the Southwest as well as his detailed and meticulously executed program for the much-needed modernization of the plant have significantly improved the overall profitability of the region. As a result of his leadership, production increased by 21% last year; the reject rate declined from 11.2% to 7.6%; and through a vigorous cost reduction program, he finished the year at 8% below budget.

One of Mr. Hood's more outstanding achievements last year was that he successfully concluded some difficult negotiations with the union when it appeared likely that a strike would be forced on us by a militant faction. More important, in return for a relatively modest increase in labor rates, he gained some significant concessions from the union with regard to scheduling and work assignments. These have increased both productivity and plant efficiency.

Mr. Hood is very thorough, detailed, and analytical in his work. He has done a good job in training and developing a loyal, competent, and company-oriented management staff, and the overall morale of the plant appears to be at an all-time high.

Identification of Growth and Development Needs

Since he is very much a "doer" and quite action oriented, Mr. Hood tends to want to carry out too many assignments

116

himself, rather than delegate some of these to his staff. Several of his key people have commented on this over a period of time, and this factor may have contributed to one or two individuals having chosen to leave the company. In addition, Mr. Hood appears to be somewhat less committed than desired to the company's OSHA and EEO programs, resulting in his failure to reach some of the previous targeted goals.

Evaluation of Future Potential

In view of his combined engineering and business education, his successful experience with our company for the past four years, his strong career drive, and his analytical problem-solving ability, Mr. Hood is unquestionably capable of advancement. Although he could remain in his present assignment for another two to three years, he would appear well qualified for the following positions should they open up:

Director of Manufacturing (Corporate Staff)
General Manager (Medium-sized Subsidiary)

Possible Replacements

Paul C. Wood, Assistant Plant Manager (Chicago Plant)
Harold J. Crawford, Production Planning Coordinator (Corporate Staff)
Peter F. Clark, Assistant Plant Manager (Cleveland-West)

Prepared by:
Vincent G. Bullard,
Vice-President–Manufacturing

In addition to its emphasis on potential for future advancement, there is another major distinction between the data furnished for the performance appraisal and for the human resources inventory. As pointed out in the preceding chapter, the performance appraisal is customarily conducted once or twice a year. Data for the human resources inventory, on the other hand, while they must be kept up to date, need not be prepared as frequently. Depending upon the rapidity of changes occurring within the company, such information should usually be reviewed every two to three years.

Needless to say, because personnel decisions resulting from the human resources inventory data are likely to be of the utmost importance to the future success of the organization, it is imperative that the original performance appraisal information on which the human resources inventory data are based be completely factual, accurate, and totally objective. For this reason, companies should make certain that their managers and executives clearly recognize the importance and multipurpose use of the performance appraisal data and provide them with sufficient indepth training in implementing the appraisal process.

As is the case with information supplied by the company's consulting management psychologist, managers from their perspective can contribute significantly to the total human resources inventory system by providing comprehensive evaluations of key individuals' current work performance, identification of their growth and development needs, and assessments of their future potential for advancement with the company.

Strategic Information Generated by a Total Human Resources Inventory System

For the past several years, many well-managed companies have developed and maintained a comprehensive and up-to-date human resources inventory listing the experience, education, and other qualifications of their key professional, managerial, and executive personnel. Such inventories greatly facilitate making objective and accurate personnel decisions regarding promotions and transfers.

Modern electronic data processing technology makes it

quite possible to store and retrieve vital personnel data with relative ease, thus providing management with a highly valuable information system. Data about an employee that are customarily stored in such a retrievable system include:

1. Relevant personal information.
2. Formal educational background.
3. Previous work experience.
4. Specialized training courses completed.
5. Knowledge of foreign languages or previous exposure to foreign cultures.
6. Special skills or knowledge.
7. Memberships or committee assignments in professional or business associations.
8. Patents, publications, or special honors or recognition received.
9. Special assignments completed within the company.
10. Employment history with the company.
11. Previous performance appraisal data.
12. Information related to the individual's career aspirations and preferences.

We are now able to supplement the above data with the information provided by the psychological evaluation and that furnished by the individual's manager to initiate the process of planning for the future growth and continuity of the company.

Using the Human Resources Inventory

As a result of all the personnel information that has been gathered, we are now ready to take an analytical look at the total human resources available to the company. A particularly useful way to review the quantity and caliber of an organization's current professional, managerial, and executive staff is to prepare a Management Needs Analysis. (A sample is shown in Figure 5.) Through the Management Needs Analysis, we immediately gain an accurate picture of the organization's personnel strength and the status of its key people.

Such an analysis of an organization's personnel can become even clearer by presenting the information in a more graphic form, as illustrated by Figure 6, the Management Resources Inventory. Here, as a result of both the psychological evaluation and the information supplied by each individual's superior, we can establish a rating for each person which describes overall current performance and, perhaps even more significant, potential for further advancement with the company.

Finally, in reviewing all the data that have been gathered, we can arrive at Figure 7, the Management Replacement and Succession Analysis. This is typically a fairly long document, because it will incorporate all relevant personnel information drawn from throughout a company, including the various divisions and subsidiaries. (Because of space limitations, Figure 7 is only a scaled-down version of the larger document that customarily would be prepared.)

The Management Replacement and Succession Analysis is clearly the most important document in the total Human Resources Inventory System. If all the relevant information has been properly gathered, we should now have before us a very clear picture of which key positions throughout the company will need to be filled; an anticipated date when the replacement will be needed; and of greatest importance, a list of possible replacement or succession candidates together with ratings describing their current performance and future potential.

Returning to our original organization planning analysis, we can now directly coordinate human resources

FIGURE 5.

MANAGEMENT NEEDS ANALYSIS: BREWSTER DIVISION

Position	Incumbent	Date Replacement Needed	Reason
General Manager	J. Hynes	1984	Retirement
Manager of Engineering	W. Brown	Now	Unsatisfactory Performance
Manufacturing Manager	C. Smith	1985	Possible Promotion
Sales Manager	H. Harris	1984	Early Retirement Indicated
Research Manager	———	Now	New Position to Be Filled
Industrial Relations Manager	T. Roe	1984	Possible Promotion
Accounting Manager	R. Clark	1985	Possible Promotion
Credit Manager	F. Ketcham	1988	Possible Promotion
Advertising Manager	———	Now	New Position to Be Filled

FIGURE 6.

MANAGEMENT RESOURCES INVENTORY:
BREWSTER DIVISION

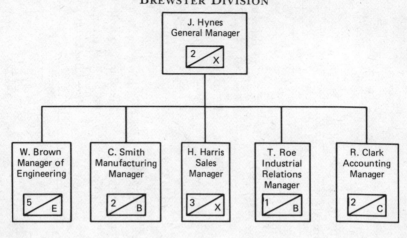

CODE

Current Performance   1. Outstanding   2. Highly Satisfactory   3. Satisfactory
                         4. Less than Satisfactory   5. Replacement Indicated
Future Potential   A. Outstanding   B. Very Good   C. Average   D. Below Average
                      E. Questionable   X. Retirement Pending

planning with strategies for the future growth and expansion of the company. Where certain individuals are being considered for eventual promotion, it may be necessary to initiate steps to prepare them more fully for their upcoming role in the organization through additional training or selected job assignments. Where it is felt that no one within the company possesses the necessary qualifications to warrant internal promotion, recruiting will need to be undertaken to locate a suitable candidate from the outside.

In this chapter, we have seen how Reality-Centered Management can be used to look ahead and ensure that a company will have the right people available for its long-range growth and continuity.

FIGURE 7.

Management Replacement and Succession

Analysis: Possible Replacement Candidates: Brewster Division

POSITION	DATE REPLACEMENT NEEDED	D. Kruger	F. Klein	T. McCarthy	W. Taylor	B. Gray	C. Jones	R. Sands	G. Forrest	T. Cody	
President	1986				1/B		1/A				Good candidates currently available
Vice-President Marketing	1984	2/B							2/B		Outside talent will need to be secured shortly
Vice-President Finance	1988		1/A							1/B	Good candidates anticipated
Vice-President Manufacturing	1989			2/B		2/B					More qualified candidates will need to be secured
Vice-President Personnel	1993							1/B			Additional candidates needed

CODE

Current Performance 1. Outstanding 2. Highly Satisfactory 3. Satisfactory 4. Less than Satisfactory 5. Replacement Indicated

Future Potential A. Outstanding B. Very Good C. Average D. Below Average E. Questionable

7
Recapitulation

&

The Current Problem and
the Future Challenge

The problem of declining productivity and work performance started slowly, almost imperceptibly, several years ago. Many thought that it was only temporary and would soon disappear. The problem did not vanish however. If anything, it has worsened to the point where it is now causing growing concern to companies, the government, and most responsible Americans.

The long-standing belief that U.S. business and industry were invincible—that no other country could even approach us, much less surpass our technological achievements and leadership—was virtually taken for granted. It was assumed that the nation's industrial machine would continue to function just as it had in the past—that it would make periodic improvements as it went along and, in so doing, advance our constantly rising standard of living. A pattern of expectations was thereby established: Most people firmly believed that a better life—even affluence, for many—lay ahead.

But something has gone drastically wrong, and it has been long in the making. The American industrial machine is ailing. It is clearly not the unchallenged force it had been for so long. With each passing day, our traditional technological superiority is being increasingly challenged by foreign competitors.

For a number of years, American employees have demanded—and generally received—higher wages and benefits, which unquestionably have enhanced their standard of living. At the same time, however, productivity has failed to keep pace with such rising labor costs, causing business and industry to lose much of their traditional competitive advantage. This can be seen from the fact that during the past decade wages have increased at an annual rate of 8.2 percent, while productivity growth has been limited to only 1.3 percent. The end result is that many American products are being outpriced, both at home and abroad.

The effects of this disastrous slippage in our industrial vitality are evident all around us. By now most Americans are aware of the powerful challenge posed by the Japanese auto industry, which is competing very successfully against U.S.-built cars not only in our own country but also in the international market. Japanese competition has virtually destroyed one American automobile manufacturer; it gravely threatens the survival of the No. 2 company; and it seriously challenges the long standing leadership of the premier company in the industry. (It is a sad commentary that a recent U.S. government study reported that most Americans themselves now believe Japanese cars are superior in quality to our own products, and that this has greatly contributed to the drastic sales decline of American-built automobiles.)

The nation's competitive decline is hardly limited to the automobile industry, although this has probably received the greatest publicity and attention. The list of industries where foreign competition has become a formidable— even threatening—factor is continually lengthening. It now includes industries where the United States has long been the leader, such as steel, textiles, footwear, and consumer electronics. *Business Week* estimates that the drop in competitiveness by American industry in recent years is of the magnitude of $125 billion in lost production and some 2 million lost jobs.

It has become increasingly clear that U.S. business and industry are not keeping up with foreign competition and are thereby losing market share, both at home and abroad. This not only threatens the nation's standard of living but also may very well jeopardize the profitability, the viability, and even the very survival of numerous U.S. companies. In addition, the decline of the U.S. industrial machine has serious implications for America's standing, power, and world role in these turbulent times.

In this connection, some observers point out that history has seen many societies and nations rise to great heights only to fall to oblivion. They say the United States may already have reached its apex and recently begun its long-range decline. However, most knowledgeable people vigorously dispute this pessimistic interpretation. While recognizing that the United States does, indeed, have some serious problems, they realize that we also possess the ability, creativity, and resources to resolve them. American business and industry is still a strong and powerful tool—in fact, it is still the undisputed leader of the world—but as Alexander Trowbridge, President of the National Association of Manufacturers, has stated, ". . . it is rusty; it needs sharpening." Clearly, the hour is late, but there is still time if vigorous, decisive steps are taken promptly.

Origin of the Productivity Problem

The problem of declining productivity is complex. No doubt numerous factors have contributed to its rise and development. Of these, most specialists agree that the following have had the most significant impact:

The decline in the rate of investment in new capital equipment.
The decline in research and development expenditures.
The increase in the cost and burden of government regulations.
The effects of inflation.
The rise in energy costs.
The decline in employee motivation and commitment to high-quality work.

In this book, we have focused exclusively on the last factor, declining motivation. While mindful of the fact that it is by no means the only cause but rather one of many, it *has*, nevertheless, been a major contributor. Few would disagree today that there has been a significant decline both in work motivation and in the quality of performance among a large segment of our employees. Every manager and indeed every reader reflecting on personal experience as a consumer can recollect numerous episodes which have clearly demonstrated the lessening of many people's will to work and work well. In its place, we have seen the rise of some highly unfortunate negative behavior patterns, including apathy, indifference and the absence of sufficient self-discipline as well as a willingness to apply oneself appropriately to the requirements of the job.

In recent years, we have seen the emergence of an entirely new, different, and—to many observers—rather disturbing attitude toward work. This attitude has had a pronounced impact both on the way work is done and on the overall quality of work performance itself. This new attitude, expressed by many employees, has reflected a concern on their part for immediate personal gratification and self-indulgence, with a concomitant decline in identification with the company and commitment to its goals and objectives. Accompanying this regrettable attitude has been the rise of a new psychology of entitlement: many employees now expect a whole array of material rewards and benefits to be provided by their employers as a matter of right, without any reciprocal productive contribution necessarily being required on their part.

Motivation and Management Revisited

The new attitude toward work held by many people conflicts sharply with long-established concepts about employee motivation and work behavior in which American managers and executives have been solidly indoctrinated for the past 20 years. Applied psychology had painted them a completely different picture.

According to the very popular and long-accepted theories, the overwhelming majority of people were supposed to have an almost inherent desire to work productively and contribute to the progress of their companies. In addition, the motivational psychologists have long claimed that most employees have both the desire and the capability to participate actively with management in decision making as it affects their jobs. As a result, if management wants to fully utilize its human resources, a participative leadership approach should significantly improve the company's operations.

The question—to which this book has attempted to respond—is If the motivational psychologists are really correct in their explanation of employee work motivation and job behavior, why do we have such an acute productivity problem in the first place?

Essentially, in my opinion, the motivational psychologists are only *partially* correct in their explanation. They have overgeneralized and lost sight of the tremendous variability that exists among people. It is also quite probable that in our turbulent and rapidly changing world people themselves and their entire outlook on work have changed. The new attitudes held by many are often not conducive to increasing organizational productivity.

Traditional applied psychology has offered some very idealistic and humanistic concepts. Realistically speaking however—as many managers have learned first hand to their dismay—such concepts do not always work. More important, they simply do not consistently respond to the productivity problem. Many managers have, in short, been deluded by theories and recommendations that, on the surface, sound very practical and effective indeed but, in the final analysis, frequently prove quite unworkable.

The Case for Reality-Centered Management

This book has suggested a new framework, Reality-Centered Management, which I feel is more workable and more likely to reflect the various factors in the work situation—not as we might wish them to be, but as they in fact actually are. Instead of clinging dogmatically to any particular leadership style, I believe that managers must have a flexible approach to directing and managing people—one which will respond accurately and realistically to the specific situations in which they find themselves.

Accordingly, managers will invariably have working for them some people who are truly work-motivated and capable of engaging with them in joint decision making. With this type of employee, the managers' leadership style should clearly be more participative. At the same time, however, managers can also expect to have working for them people who are inherently less motivated toward work, and who may lack the capacity or, for that matter, even the interest to participate in the decision-making process. In such an instance, managers should assume a much more directive leadership style—one that provides such employees with the needed structure and support that will enable them to perform most effectively.

In addition, to resolve the productivity dilemma, it is necessary for business and industry to return to some of the managerial basics, which have too long been neglected. Of primary importance in this context is that all managers establish definite and appropriately high performance standards and hold their people fully accountable for attaining them. In this way, all managers will be able to contribute significantly to revitalizing their companies and raising the productivity level.

Needed: A New National Purpose

By now the majority of knowledgeable Americans have become acutely aware of the seriousness of the problem of declining productivity growth and the many dangers it poses to our standard of living and our nation's welfare. In the last year or two, a growing realization has swept the country that something has gone drastically wrong with our business and industrial machine, and we are in the process of losing our competitive edge to foreign competitors. Most people recognize that the productivity problem is enormously complex and multifaceted, and a vast effort will be needed if we are to successfully resolve it.

I believe that the productivity problem is of such magnitude that finding a successful solution will call for a major commitment from the nation's various institutions as well as from all Americans. Indeed, the challenge suggests that the time is right for a new national purpose such as the United States has not had since the days of the

Second World War. No one has ever questioned our country's capacity for productivity and goal achievement when the nation is truly committed to a purpose.

This book has already indicated the concrete steps that business and industry as well as each individual can take to add their respective contributions to the total effort. However, if the drive for productivity improvement is to take on the aspect of a national purpose, the support of all the country's various institutions must be enlisted. In this regard, labor unions, which clearly have a tremendous stake in seeing that the decline in productivity growth is dramatically reversed, can play a major role. Schools, colleges, universities and, yes, the entertainment media, too can all make vital contributions by helping to promote appropriate attitudes conducive to productivity improvement. Finally, our religious institutions and our homes can have a significant impact by helping to instill a firm commitment to high-quality work performance.

A satisfactory level of industrial productivity is, in the final analysis, what provides the foundation for full employment, economic prosperity, and national security. Beyond this, a vigorous economy is a prerequisite for the country's pursuit of such broader—and highly desirable—goals as social justice, environmental protection, and an enhanced quality of life, about which so much has been written in recent years. Hence, a commitment to productivity improvement is a goal with which all Americans can identify and wholeheartedly support—a truly national purpose.

Appendix

ॐ

Sample Psychological Evaluations *

MARTIN T. WILSON
FOR APPLIED TECHNOLOGY, INC.

As a result of a clinical interview supplemented by appropriate intelligence and psychological tests, we are pleased to submit to you in confidence our professional evaluation of the qualifications of Mr. Martin T. Wilson for the position of President of Applied Technology, Inc.

Recommendation
On balance, Mr. Wilson is considered a highly satisfactory but not totally "ready" candidate for the position in question. Accordingly, he is given an overall rating of "2" on a scale on which "1" represents outstanding qualifications, "2" is above average, "3" is marginal, and "4" is poor. Mr. Wilson can therefore be given very serious consideration for promotion to this key assignment.

Summary
Viewed predominantly from an intermediate to a longer-term perspective, we regard Mr. Wilson to be of true executive caliber: He is an individual who unquestionably has all the essential management skills and attributes

* Although these are actual evaluations, the names have been changed.

needed to develop into a highly effective executive. Indeed, his key qualifications are quite formidable. He possesses an unusually high intelligence; he has had a first-rate education; and he demonstrates most of the interpersonal and motivational qualities necessary to play an important management role in a major corporation.

Mr. Wilson's track record of proven business accomplishments is equally impressive. He has had some eight years of responsible hands-on operating experience with General Electric Company, and even more significant, he has had a major part in the successful growth and development of your newly acquired Computer Components Division.

However, we would like to call attention to the fact that, in our evaluation, Mr. Wilson has never been exposed to the same *scope, magnitude,* or *complexity* of assignments that would inevitably await him were he to take on the presidency of Applied Technology. For example, until now the greatest number of people for which he has been responsible was at General Electric: approximately 125 employees. At Computer Components we understand there is presently a complement of about 70.

More important, Mr. Wilson has generally been involved in operations having a dollar volume a fraction of that of your company. Furthermore, as a rule, he has been concerned with only a *single* operation rather than the multiple operations of a highly diversified, multifaceted company comprised of many different divisions with diverse problems and challenges.

This is *not* to say we would expect Mr. Wilson to fail were he to assume the position of chief operating officer of Applied Technology. However, before being placed in the position in question, we would ideally like to see Mr. Wilson get several additional years of notably broader and more diversified operating experience, preferably in the

Applied Technology environment, in order to significantly round out his business knowledge and experience.

For example—once again, ideally speaking—we would recommend a three- to four-year period during which Mr. Wilson might serve as executive vice-president of Applied Technology and, more important, have the benefit of working very closely with your present board chairman and president as well as with the various divisional presidents. Such a period would serve as an optimal preparation that unquestionaby would fully develop him and pave the way for him to take on this critical assignment.

In essence, then, we see Mr. Wilson as having unusual talent as well as great potential that unquestionably can be developed. He is not, however, what we would call "an instant corporate president." Therefore, were he to be put into this position now, we feel he would require a certain amount of concentrated attention, guidance, and direction from Applied Technology management at the very highest level. Such attention could compensate for his lack of greater and more diversified, in-depth management experience until such time as this relative deficiency is removed.

Personal Background
Mr. Wilson, an only child, was brought up in Chicago and is 39 years old. His father, who died last year, was a real estate salesman who apparently never achieved any real business success. As a result, the family circumstances were often relatively modest. Mr. Wilson was an active, involved, and fairly energetic youngster who in the course of his family upbringing was exposed to most of the traditional middle-class values and standards.

No doubt as a result of his very superior intellectual capacity, Mr. Wilson was an outstanding student in high school and, because of his high academic standing, won a scholarship to the University of Minnesota. Here he majored in chemical engineering and was graduated in 1963 fairly close to the top of his class. While at the university, he took part in a wide range of campus activities and, for a time, served as president of the student body.

Having been a member of the Naval ROTC on campus, shortly after graduation Mr. Wilson was called to active duty and served two years as an officer on a destroyer escort. After being separated, he decided to continue his education. In 1965, he enrolled at the Stanford Graduate School of Business, where he specialized in marketing and production, and from which in 1967 he received his M.B.A. degree, graduating in the top 10 percent of his class.

Toward the end of his M.B.A. program at Stanford, Mr. Wilson was offered employment with the Major Appliance Division of General Electric. He joined the company in 1967 as assistant to the general manager of the division's Dallas plant and subsequently undertook a variety of operational assignments in the field of plant management.

More specifically, Mr. Wilson's first opportunity to run a plant of his own was as general manager of General Electric's Tulsa plant, which when he arrived was not a particularly profitable one. He remained there for some 3 years, during which a measure of progress was made, and subsequently took on a larger plant at Indianapolis for still another 3½ years.

Early in 1975, Mr. Wilson was approached by Mr. Thomas Harrell, a former colleague with whom he had worked for a time at General Electric. Mr. Harrell was at that point in the process of forming his own company in San Jose, Computer Components, Inc., which Applied Technology has recently acquired. Sensing a challenging growth opportunity, Mr. Wilson joined Computer Components. His initial responsibility was to develop the company's marketing program overseas.

During the past five years, Mr. Wilson has been quite

deeply involved in all aspects of Computer Components operating management, including production, engineering, and marketing, both in the United States and overseas. In the course of these years, he was successively appointed vice-president and executive vice-president, and since the acquisition of the company has been serving as president of the division.

Regarding his personal life, Mr. Wilson is married to a woman three years his junior whom he met while both were students at the University of Minnesota. Mrs. Wilson is a career woman in her own right and is currently employed as an English teacher in a local junior high school. The couple have two girls, ages 14 and 9, and reside in their own home in Palo Alto. Although the majority of his leisure time is focused on family activities, Mr. Wilson nevertheless takes part in a variety of social, community, and local business functions and activities as well.

Psychological Evaluation

In acquiring Computer Components, we think that your company has simultaneously acquired a most capable executive in Mr. Wilson. At the outset, it should be said that he is an exceedingly intelligent person, whose intellectual capability surpasses that of the vast majority of business executives.

Specifically, Mr. Wilson has a very keen, logical, and practical mind; he is capable of engaging in substantial critical and analytical thinking, both conceptually and quantitatively; and he can evaluate a given situation, come to a correct decision, and subsequently chart a definite and appropriate course of action. Similarly, Mr. Wilson is a very well organized and systematic individual who is adept at keeping his priorities in proper order. He is quite effective in coordinating both people and activities toward attaining established organizational goals and targets.

In the interpersonal area, Mr. Wilson equals his intellectual qualities. He is an informal, straightforward, and down-to-earth executive who can readily gain the respect and trust of his people. Indeed, he places great value on building an effective and competent team of conscientious, dedicated, and self-motivated individuals on whom he can rely to assist him in meeting essential organizational objectives. He emphasizes intracompany coordination and teamwork and prides himself on his ability to build a smoothly functioning, integrated organization.

To a great extent, Mr. Wilson is basically a somewhat private person. He is not inherently gregarious or outgoing. In fact, if anything, he leans somewhat toward the retiring side. As a rule, he does not get too close to too many people.

Nevertheless, in his business dealings, Mr. Wilson projects the image of a poised and sophisticated executive; yet his manner is quite casual and completely unpretentious. At the same time, however, Mr. Wilson sets high personal standards for himself and expects that his associates will rise to the occasion and respond equally well to further the success of the company.

In this context, there is a degree of controlled but appropriate business aggressiveness in Mr. Wilson. It should be pointed out that he is not reluctant to assume a sufficiently forceful and dominant posture when a situation so requires. Indeed, in recent years at Computer Components, Mr. Wilson has probably had to learn to develop additional self-confidence in order to keep pace with the company's dynamic growth as well as with his own expanding responsibilities—a process which we believe is still going on at this time.

Another of Mr. Wilson's more outstanding managerial talents is his ability to communicate effectively. Essentially, he is a rather verbal and articulate person with good expressive skills which enable him to convey an idea to others in a convincing, authoritative, and persuasive manner, thereby gaining support and acceptance for his viewpoints and proposals.

Even though Mr. Wilson generally prefers to think and plan for the near to intermediate term, we nevertheless assess him to be a rather ambitious person with decidedly high long-range career aspirations. Were he to remain as President of Computer Components, no doubt the job would more than fully satisfy him for the next four to five years.

Beyond that time, however, Mr. Wilson is very likely to get somewhat restless and, at that point, seek greater stimulation in a different endeavor. Indeed, it is this very factor that has caused Mr. Wilson to actively explore with you the immediate opportunity to take on the presidency of Applied Technology, even though he probably feels that such a position, from his personal perspective, might be a bit premature at this juncture.

Mr. Wilson also qualifies quite readily psychologically for a high executive position. He demonstrates appropriate behavioral flexibility as well as the capacity to respond effectively to changing business conditions. He is able to absorb typical stress, tension, and pressure without having it impair either his judgment or his actions. He has a well-balanced, positive outlook on life. Indeed, he is a very solid citizen, somewhat on the conservative and restrained side, and is in no way given to rash, impulsive, or precipitous behavior.

Quite clearly, at this point in his life, Mr. Wilson is at a crossroads. While he did not personally seek the position as President of Applied Technology, now that the idea has been presented to him, he is very much interested and quite enthusiastic at the possibility of taking on the assignment.

Simultaneously, however, Mr. Wilson places great emphasis on the well-being of his family and realizes that his wife—who is currently professionally employed in

California and, recognizing the current labor market, could not be assured of comparable employment in this area—might not quite share his enthusiasm at the contemplated relocation. Mr. Wilson feels that any such decision must be made by both himself and his wife, and significantly, he would not wish to unduly influence her toward an affirmative decision. We feel, however, that if your company were to extend a definite offer to Mr. Wilson, the family—perhaps after some deliberation—would in all probability agree to the move.

In closing, we generally regard Mr. Wilson as a highly competent, up-and-coming business executive. It is obvious that in his positions to date he has proved himself quite able—a track record he will undoubtedly continue.

In the Summary section of this report, we have spelled out our reservations about Mr. Wilson with respect to the position currently under discussion. As we have pointed out, ideally, we would prefer a candidate for this assignment with a somewhat broader, more diversified, and multidivisional experience than that currently offered by Mr. Wilson.

Nevertheless, if you do not feel our reservations are sufficiently serious and, more important, are prepared to give Mr. Wilson the time to fully develop into the position, we believe that he will substantially meet your expectations in this assignment.

PETER SANFORD
FOR UNIVERSAL CHEMICAL CORPORATION

As the result of a clinical interview, supplemented by appropriate intelligence and psychological tests, we are pleased to submit to you in confidence our professional evaluation of the qualifications of Mr. Peter Sanford for the position of assistant to the president of your company, the Universal Chemical Corporation.

Recommendation

Mr. Sanford is not considered particularly promising as a candidate for the position in question. He is given an overall rating of "3" on a scale on which "1" represents outstanding qualifications, "2" is above average, "3" is marginal, and "4" is poor. Therefore Mr. Sanford is not recommended for employment.

Summary

Despite the fact that Mr. Sanford is truly brilliant and has a great intellectual capacity and could no doubt make a most useful contribution to certain organizations, we do not think he would ever really satisfy your expectations in the position of assistant to the president.

Fundamentally, the problem is that the "fit" between Mr. Sanford's personality and that of your company is not particularly good. Despite his impressive intellectual capacity, Mr. Sanford is not mentally facile. He is a relatively slow, ponderous, and roundabout thinker. Neither his verbal presentations nor his negotiating skills are incisive or persuasive.

Moreover, we do not see Mr. Sanford as a particularly *action-oriented* or *decisive* individual. And while he may regard himself as a potentially successful line operating executive, we, for our part, are more inclined to think that a permanent *staff* assignment where the demands and pressures inherent in the position are not excessive would be much more suited to Mr. Sanford's personality and temperament.

Lastly, to some extent, Mr. Sanford does not impress us as possessing that much business maturity nor, in our judgment, has his past work experience been distinctive. Recognizing your company's demanding expectations— especially with regard to the position in question—we do not feel that, at the age of 34, Mr. Sanford can show particularly outstanding accomplishments.

In short, in our opinion, Mr. Sanford's qualifications do not come close enough to Universal's traditionally high standards. We suggest that you pass him by in favor of an appreciably more promising candidate.

Personal Background

Born and brought up amid comfortable and rather privileged circumstances in northeastern England, the son of the successful owner of a medium-size retail shoe chain, Mr. Sanford is currently 34 years old. He received his secondary education at the well-known Eton School. After graduation, he traveled throughout Europe for six months, and in 1957 he enrolled at Cambridge University. He majored in engineering science and in 1961 received a B.A. degree.

After another six months of travel, Mr. Sanford embarked upon his professional career. Trading on his educational background, he accepted employment with Halliburton & Partners, a London-based firm of consulting engineers, where for the next five and a half years he was involved in the design and construction of various types of water installation facilities.

Toward the spring of 1967, Mr. Sanford began to feel that he needed a greater degree of more generalized business experience. Consequently, he resigned from his engineering position. He traveled for another six months, this time to North Africa and the Mediterranean area, and then decided to emigrate to the United States. In November of 1967, he took on a job similar to the one he had held in England with Harris, McCarthy & Simpson, a firm of consulting engineers located in New York City.

The nature of his work with this firm was comparable to that in his previous position. After approximately a year and a half, Mr. Sanford became disenchanted with his job and decided to resign. His salary was then $12,500.

Mr. Sanford went through his by now customary six- to eight-month period of travel, then came to the conclusion that what he wanted to do next was to pursue graduate work in business. Accordingly, he enrolled at the Graduate School of Business at UCLA—primarily because he wanted to live in California—and in June of 1971 he received an M.B.A. degree. He returned to Europe for more travel and, in November of 1971, accepted employment in New York with Texaco. Since that time, he has served as a planning analyst in the Marketing Planning section of Texaco's International Division, where his current salary is $23,500.

Several months ago, Mr. Sanford came to the conclusion that he does not really wish to stay in the oil industry. He feels that the outlook in this business is not particularly promising. Also, he feels that his growth progress at Texaco is apt to be too slow to suit him.

On the personal side, Mr. Sanford is single and rents an apartment in Manhattan. His game plan is to obtain a position that within two or three years would give him enough experience to move into a position of line responsibility in the field of operating management.

Psychological Evaluation

As previously indicated, we are most impressed with Mr. Sanford's level of intelligence. He achieved the highest scores we have ever seen on our firm's various tests measuring mental ability. We are inclined to describe Mr. Sanford's intellectual capacity as virtually unlimited. Accordingly, we think he could undertake just about any assignment given to him and come up with logical and clearly formulated conclusions and recommendations.

However, brilliant as Mr. Sanford may be, we do not think that he would fit the particular bill as assistant to your company's president. In one word, we feel that Mr. Sanford and Universal Chemical would be "mismatched." We do not think Mr. Sanford's personality and basic temperament are suited to your company's pace and tempo.

Fundamentally, as we see him, Mr. Sanford is insufficiently action oriented to give an adequate account of himself within the Universal Chemical environment. Despite his indisputable intellectual ability, Mr. Sanford is not an incisive thinker, nor is he particularly decisive in his actions. Indeed, even though he undeniably is quite personable—poised, urbane, and cosmopolitan in manner—he is also inclined to be professorial and too academic in his approach to business. More specifically, he is not a keen, rapid, or particularly alert thinker. At times, his memory is somewhat faulty, he is often slow to react to a given problem or situation, and he frequently cogitates and hesitates ponderously before arriving at a conclusion.

We also feel that Mr. Sanford's communication skills could profit considerably from sharpening. He is much too expansive verbally, takes a long time to get to the point, and frequently loses his listener along the way. Therefore, we feel that Mr. Sanford would not always be as successful as he should be in persuading or convincing others on a given point, nor do we think that he would be notably effective in overall business negotiations.

In many ways, too, especially recognizing the particular position at stake, we feel that Mr. Sanford lacks sufficient business maturity and prior practical work exposure. To some extent, even though he is already 34, he still has the outlook and perspective of the typical recent graduate of a prestigious, ivy-league business school.

Moreover, we do not feel that Mr. Sanford is quite as settled or directed in his business career as he might be— again noting the assignment for which he is being considered. His track record, in our estimation, is not overly spectacular and is basically limited to seven years of engineering experience supplemented by less than two years as a marketing analyst at Texaco.

Conclusion
In conclusion, then, were he to join your company, we do not think that Mr. Sanford would achieve the kind of results you would expect from him. Intelligent as he may be, we believe that his personality and temperament would prevent him from functioning as effectively as anticipated, either as assistant to your president or as a potential line operating executive, in the foreseeable future. As a result, we feel that a negative recommendation is called for.

Bibliography

Alber, Antone F., "The Real Cost of Job Enrichment." *Business Horizons,* February 1979, pp. 60–72.

Argyris, Chris, *Integrating the Individual and the Organization.* New York: John Wiley & Sons, 1964.

Fein, M., "Job Enrichment: A Reevaluation." *Sloan Management Review,* Winter 1974, pp. 69–88.

Ford Foundation, *A Work Experiment: Six Americans in a Swedish Plant.* New York: The Ford Foundation, 1976.

Ford, Robert N., *Motivation Through the Work Itself.* New York: American Management Associations, 1969.

Hackman, J. Richard, and Oldham, Greg R., *Work Redesign.* Reading, Mass.: Addison-Wesley, 1980.

Herzberg, Frederick, "One More Time: How Do You Motivate Employees?" *Harvard Business Review,* January–February 1968, pp. 53–62.

Herzberg, Frederick, *Work and the Nature of Man.* Cleveland: World Publishing Company, 1966.

House, Robert J., and Wigdor, Lawrence A., "Herzberg's Dual-Factor Theory of Job Satisfaction and Motivation. A Review of the Evidence and a Criticism." *Personnel Psychology,* Winter 1967, pp. 369–89.

Howard, Ann, and Bray, Douglas W., "Career Motivation in Mid-Life Managers." Paper presented at the American Psychological Association Annual Convention, Montreal, Canada, September 1980.

Howard, Ann, and Bray, Douglas W., "Continuities and Discontinuities Between Two Generations of Bell System Managers." Paper presented at the American Psychological Association Annual Convention, Montreal, Canada, September 1980.

Kerr, Clark, and Rosow, Jerome M., *Work in America: The Decade Ahead.* New York: Van Nostrand Reinhold, 1979.

Likert, Rensis, *The Human Organization.* New York: McGraw-Hill, 1967.

Maslow, A. H., *Motivation and Personality.* 2nd ed. New York: Harper & Row, 1970.

McGregor, Douglas, *The Human Side of Enterprise.* New York: McGraw-Hill, 1960.

Myers, M. Scott, *Every Employee A Manager.* New York: McGraw-Hill, 1970.

"The Reindustrialization of America." *Business Week,* June 30, 1980, pp. 56–142.

Rush, Harold M. F., *Job Design for Motivation.* New York: The Conference Board, 1971.

Schrank, Robert, *Ten Thousand Working Days.* Cambridge, Mass.: MIT Press, 1978.

Stanton, Erwin S., *Successful Personnel Recruiting and Selection.* New York: AMACOM, 1977.

Winpisinger, William W., "Job Satisfaction: A Union Response." *American Federationist,* February 1973, pp. 8–10.

Work in America. Report of a Special Task Force to the Secretary of Health, Education and Welfare. Boston: MIT Press, 1972.

Yankelovich, Daniel, "We Need New Motivational Tools." *Industry Week,* August 6, 1979, pp. 61–68.

Index